WHISTLING GIRL

WHISTLING GIRL

HELEN LAWRENSON

DOUBLEDAY & COMPANY, INC., GARDEN CITY, NEW YORK 1978

Parts of Chapter 4 first appeared in *Cosmopolitan* and in *Playgirl* (July 1974). The author gratefully acknowledges permission to reprint.

ISBN: 0-385-11573-3
Library of Congress Catalog Card Number 77–89682
Printed in the United States of America
First Edition

Whistling girls and crowing hens
Always come to some bad ends.

Old Saying

WHISTLING GIRL

Chapter One

—————◆—————

YOU CAN ALWAYS GET A DRINK IN
A WHOREHOUSE

The first time I was ever in a whorehouse was in Havana back in the Thirties. I was on a winter cruise, taking a holiday from my job as a magazine editor, and the ship made a three-day stop at the beautiful, shining Cuban capital, where I was taken in tow by an elderly expatriate Bostonian named Kendrigan, an erudite faculty member of the University of Havana to whom a mutual friend had written, asking him to show me the city. It turned out his idea of a guided tour was not historic monuments or scenic spots but cockfights, blue movies, waterfront bars, marijuana parties, tough dancehalls, brothels—in none of which had I ever set foot before. I took to them like a duck to water.

He didn't tell me we were going to visit a bordello, and this one, on Lamparilla Street, looked like any ordinary house. It was not until a maid ushered us into the reception room, where Kendrigan introduced me to a group of girls in kimonas, that it dawned on me. For a while we sat in the inevitable Cuban rocking chairs, sipping a soda pop aptly called *gaseosa* and chatting conventionally: Where was my home? What did I think of Havana? How long was I going to stay? Aside from their attire, the girls were as decorous as if we were at a church social. They seemed even more curious about me than I was about them. I was young and good-looking and I was wearing a white flannel trouser suit I had bought at Abercrombie & Fitch for the cruise. They had

never seen a woman in such an outfit and indeed at that time neither had I, except in photographs of Marlene Dietrich. They also
admired my Molyneux perfume, and one of the girls, Lucrezia,
said it smelled like fresh violets. After a half hour of this sort of
amiably polite conversation, Lucrezia and another girl, who had
been whispering to Kendrigan, got up and led us into a bedroom
where there were two more rocking chairs and a large bed with a
crucifix on the wall over the headboard, traditional decor for
Latin prostitutes. Kendrigan and I sat on the chairs while the girls
sprawled on the bed in a nude coil, their moans of simulated
pleasure interrupted by giggling fits as they beckoned me to join
in the frolic. I refused, thanking them in my best Spanish. I suppose Kendrigan may have hoped that I would tear off my clothes
and leap into bed with them, but I didn't have the slightest urge
to do so and never have in all the similar exhibitions I've
witnessed since then. It was considered chic and amusing in those
years to visit a cat house to see a circus or daisy chain, as the exhibition was called, but it never titillated me one whit. I was neither
shocked nor embarrassed. It just seemed silly to sit there staring at
two or three girls—sometimes with a man thrown into the mêlée
—and anyway I could never see well what was going on because
I'm terribly nearsighted and I certainly wasn't going to put on my
glasses. Then, too, I've never been sure of the proper etiquette.
Does one utter comments of approbation or encouragement? "Go
it, girls!" or "Bravo!" Does one applaud the performers at the
end? I've always felt like saying, "That was very nice, girls. Now
you must come and see me sometime." *Olé!*

Kendrigan evidently thought his presence was inhibiting me, so
he left the room, ignoring my cries of "Hey! Don't go off and
leave me here!" As soon as he had gone, the girls stopped their
puppet show, sat up and began to talk. "Don't you like us?" Lucrezia asked. "Don't you think me pretty?" "I think you're beautiful," I said truthfully. She looked like Norma Shearer, the old-
time movie star. Turquoise eyes, chiseled nose, classic lips, the
same pure line of profile. I told her this and she said her favorite
movie actress was Joan Crawford. When she learned that I had
actually met Joan, she dropped all professional pretense and plied
me with questions. When Kendrigan tiptoed back into the room
he found, not an orgy, but me holding the whores spellbound

with tales of Hollywood. We all shook hands and I left, promising to come again should I ever return to Cuba. I kept my word. I went back a couple of times on subsequent trips, for a drink and a chat. Lucrezia welcomed me like an old school days friend. The last time I saw her she told me she was saving her money to get married. She had already bought her wedding dress and she opened the doors of a large mahogany wardrobe to show me. There, hanging between a scarlet silk kimona and a transparent black negligee, was a bridal gown of white satin and lace, with a long tulle veil attached to a coronet of artificial orange blossoms. She tried it on for me to see and admire. "If business is good," she said, "I'll have enough for a nice church wedding in a few months." I wished her happiness, and I meant it.

Ever since, I've always gotten along fine with whores in Cuba, Mexico, Panama, the Canary Islands, Europe, America, wherever I've met them. We talk about clothes and our favorite movie stars. They know I'm not interested in them sexually, either as participant or voyeur, that I'm not slumming, that I don't want anything from them. I'm not a sociologist or a social worker or a reformer. I'm not a medical or a psychological freak. I'm not a reporter doing a feature series on vice, or even a researcher of some kind, getting material for novel, play or thesis. I accept them on a friendly, equal basis; and they accept me. They're not after my money or my body. Their attitude toward me has always been trusting, respectful, even protective.

I'm not talking about upper-echelon courtesans like the "international playgirls," status symbols for multimillionaires, who become celebrities in their own right by fucking maharajahs, Arab potentates, princes, heads of state (including American presidents), and various assorted tycoons. Nor do I mean those sleek $100-an-hour dazzlers, the call girls you can take off your income tax as a business expense for entertaining prospective clients. Neither them nor the part-time hookers, *Belle de Jour* style, in Long Island suburban vice rings, all married, some with children, moonlighting prostitutes once characterized by a Nassau County district attorney as "typical housewives who live in split-level houses of suburbia." *Belle de Jackson Heights.* I've never experienced any desire to be a whore, even in fantasy, and I'm sure this type of pin money entrepreneurs, along with the super-*poule-de-luxe* girls, would be suspicious of me and possibly hostile, although I've been at least on speaking terms with a few of the latter, including one upper-bracket doxy I met in Mexico City. She called herself Diane Harris and was dubbed Golden Girl by the American press because an assistant district attorney described her in court as "the golden girl of café society" during the New York trial of Mickey Jelke (Minot F. Jelke, Jr., referred to as "the oleomargarine heir) on charges of compulsory prostitution. Golden Girl, a material witness, was a platinum blonde with an innocent face and delicate beauty. She appeared in court wearing an obviously expensive mink stole and a magnificent gold bracelet studded with pearls and diamonds. She sobbed unceasingly when the court was told that she had been a prostitute, had toured Europe with "a wealthy foreign tycoon," went to Egypt to meet King Farouk (his overthrow put the kibosh on that little caper), had been given an $8,000 Alfa Romeo by a Greek millionaire (she kept it in Rome, paying a chauffeur $600 a month to stand by) and had a small fortune in jewels stashed away in Zurich, plus cash in Paris. Released on bail of $25,000, she fled to Mexico, where she soon found a rich protector. I met her at a party and she took a liking to me, somewhat to my embarrassment as at that particular time I was being photographed, interviewed and written about in the Mexican press. Every time a photographer showed up in a night-club where we both were, Golden Girl threw her arms around me and there I'd be, idiotically trying to extricate myself from her embrace. In view of the fact that she was the object of an international police search, I was reluctant to appear her bosom pal. She had no physical designs on me. She just wanted a chum. She prattled incessantly, with girlish vanity, about her career, in which she had risen from the ranks, apparently through sheer merit. I heard all about the time she was approached by the representative of a famous Mideast ruler. The next day she enrolled at Berlitz for a crash course in Arabic and soon she was en route to the Persian Gulf, returning three months later with a sizable bounty in jewels as a little token of the monarch's esteem. "I've had some weirdos in my day, honey," she told me. "There's this Texas oil millionaire. Every few weeks or so, he sends for me and you know what? We check in at a hotel and he gives me a wad of money and I have to go out and buy him a bra, panties, garter belt, stockings, dresses, all frilly and sexy, and then he puts them on in front of me and prances up and down the room. That's all. He never touches me. Then he pays me a couple of grand and that's it until next time. Then there's this other one, a blind guy, who said he'd pay me a thousand dollars if I'd pee in his mouth. Can you imagine?" "Did you?" I asked. "Certainly not!" she said indignantly. "I wouldn't be that uncouth."

She was childlike and always good-natured. I was sorry to read in a newspaper five years later that she was found dead in Houston, nude, with blood on the corner of her mouth. Despite the mysterious circumstances, her death was officially attributed to liver failure, alcoholism and morphine. She was only thirty.

When I was a young woman in New York the most stylish whorehouse was run by Polly Adler on the Upper East Side, where ithyphallic revels were attended by members of the Social Register and those in top-notch financial, literary, theatrical and political circles, as well as more affluent gangsters like Lucky Luciano and Dutch Schultz. Polly claimed she turned away thirty or forty girls for every one she took on. She referred to the inmates of her lupanar as "my kids" ("They're go-getters, my kids!" she said proudly) and taught them manners and grammar. Condé Nast was one of her patrons and he once took me there as a surprise treat, I guess, but he wasted his money. Group sex was never my cup of tea. I've always been strictly Noah's Ark: one male, one female. I remember Polly as a tiny woman, under five feet tall, with dark hair and eyes. She had emigrated from Russia at the age of twelve and at fourteen was working in a paper factory for three dollars a week but decided that this was no way to make a fortune. She became a procuress with the help of a Prohibition bootlegger.

The establishment to which Condé took me was luxuriously furnished and looked like—well, it looked like an expensive whorehouse: green satin draperies, rose quartz and jade lamps, a mixture of French, Egyptian and Chinese antique furniture, an elaborate tapestry showing Venus and Vulcan at dalliance. After the customary ritual of courteous small talk and drinks, there was the usual circus performance, with me complaining sotto voce, "If you had told me where we were going, you'd have saved money," and Condé hissing "Shhh!" Then a naked young man drew me to the bed while a girl took charge of Condé. The latter two were soon entwined, huffing and puffing like The Little Engine That Could, but I pushed away my young man, who had pulled up my skirt and was diligently attempting cunnilingus or, as the current slang term was, "muff-diving." "Don't bother," I said. I told him I thought he looked familiar. It turned out he used to work in drag at the Club Richmond, an off-and-on haunt of mine, and we launched into a gossipy session of whatever-became-of-so-and-so. "I mean the one who looked like Jean Harlow." "Oh, *her.* My dear, that bitch went to Frisco. Say, do you remember the one who looked like Gail Patrick? Oooh, didn't he wear the most gorgeous gowns? Looked like he stepped out of V*ogue.*"

We sat there on the side of the bed, happily chatting away, oblivious to the heaving and panting going on right beside us. That finally came to an end, the girl got up and left, my friend shook hands, said, "Well, I certainly enjoyed meeting you, Miss," and also departed, leaving Condé and me in peace. He didn't seem to mind that I was such a party pooper. I think perhaps he was flattered that I preferred to be alone with him. About a year later Polly was arrested in a vice crackdown and her list of patrons confiscated. Prominent men left town in droves, shaking in their boots. Condé got Bernard M. Baruch to call the police commissioner to keep his name out of court and the papers.

So much for the high-class hetaerae. The girls I've found most friendly, by and large, are not the classy tarts but the common ordinary garden variety, the ones who work as streetwalkers or in low-down brothels or who pick up their tricks in sailors' bars or similar *boîtes* often displaying a sign, Rooms Upstairs, like the International Restaurant on the New York waterfront, where I spent a gala New Year's Eve with friends and got along so well with the top resident whore, a buxom, hard-eyed, peroxide blonde, that she offered me a job there, saying solicitously, "I'll treat you like you was my own sister and show you the ropes." We were chatting cozily together because she and I were the only ones still comparatively sober as the sun came up. The other members of my party, all male, were in various stages of passing out, save for one merchant seaman who had joined us and who had visited one of the Rooms Upstairs with Sophie, an experience that seemed to have depressed him, as for the next hour he sat with head in hands,

muttering over and over at intervals. "It took me twenty-one minutes to get my gun off." I wondered how he timed it so exactly but
decided to be tactful and refrain from comment.

My interest in the profession began as literary and romantic,
sparked off while I was still at Vassar by books like *Nana*, *Rox-
ana the Fortunate Mistress*, Stephen Crane's *Maggie: A Girl of
the Streets* (which he wrote when he was twenty, a student at
Syracuse University who had never laid eyes on the Bowery, the lo-
cale of the book). Intellectually eager to investigate Life-in-the-
Raw as described in these and similar classics, a schoolmate and I
persuaded two Italian bootleggers from Poughkeepsie to drive us
to Albany's red-light district, then known as The Gut, where we
stared in naïve awe at the rows of bagnios. We had been steadily
sampling a Prohibition product from our escorts' hip flasks and,
thereby emboldened, prodded one of the bootleggers into fetching
the madam of a house out to the car on the pretext that he had
two girls who wanted jobs. She peered at us dubiously, inquired
our age—we were both eighteen—and advised us against the life
of her world, warning us, "All you get in the end is a big hole."
Then she asked us, "Can you French?" We didn't have the
faintest idea what she really meant but replied enthusiastically,
"Yes indeed." After she went back in her house, saying she didn't
think we were the type, one of us asked innocently, "Why did she
want to know if we can speak French?" The bootleggers stared at
each other, speechless. They knew we were from Vassar; they certainly knew we weren't on the make (we were both virgins); they
treated us with deference, but I doubt if they had realized just
how unsophisticated we were, steeped in our academic aura. Anyway, they didn't explain what the madam meant and if they had,
we probably wouldn't have believed them, as we'd never heard of
such a practice. Take it in your *mouth?* We would have thought
they made it up.

"Never mind, girls," said one of the bootleggers as we headed
back toward Poughkeepsie. "We could always set you up in a
house across the street and my pal and I would keep running in
and out so folks'd think you was popular and had a lot of customers." He was funny and nice. They never made any passes at
us and it didn't even occur to us that they might. I suppose it was
an unusual experience for them, just as it was for us, or perhaps

they thought we were a little dotty. I don't think so, though. I
have been in a lot of exceedingly tough dives and I have always
found that if you behave yourself, treat people as equals, act naturally and courteously without trying to attract attention, you are
never molested in any way.

"Did anyone ever meet a real whore?" asked Buff Cobb, Irwin
S. Cobb's daughter, one time in the late Thirties when a group of
us were at a cocktail party. "I have," I said. "Dozens." I'm sure
nobody believed me, although it was true. The first one I actually
met ran a speakeasy in Syracuse, New York. She had been a street-
walker before her marriage and every once in a while she went
back to hustling, either because of a tiff with her husband or just
for the hell of it. She had a marvelous complexion, large hazel
eyes and a quiet, demure manner. I have never met a whore in
real life who went sashaying around in black fish-net stockings
and skintight dress, swinging her hips and talking tough, as they
were usually portrayed on stage and screen, like Lenore Ulric in
Kiki, for example, or Joan Crawford playing Sadie Thompson in
Rain. It has been my experience that they dress more or less like
other women; they make an effort to act ladylike; and they are apt
to bridle huffily if strangers use words they consider are not "gen-
teel." "No one can use that kind of language in front of *my*
house!" said the madam in The Gut that long-ago Albany night,
when one of the bootleggers burned his finger on a match and
said "Shit!"

Most of my acquaintance has been with Latin American prostitutes, possibly more conscious of an outcaste status and happy to
be treated as ladies by another woman, especially one obviously of
the straight world and with no ax to grind—just friendly social-
izing. What began as bookish curiosity on my part soon became a
practical adjunct to conviviality. It used to be a joke among men
that when caught in a brothel they'd say, "I just stopped in to buy
the girls a drink." With me, it was the truth. In a lifetime of
drinking for fun, I have found all over the world that when the
bars and other night spots have closed, you can always get a drink
in a whorehouse.

I'm not going through the long list of the many friendly trol-
lops I've met throughout the years. I've never encountered any
who showed any resentment toward me or who tried to clip me

or con me. A few stand out from the others, either because of themselves or the circumstances. They all treated me decently, when in many cases they could have done otherwise.

Foreign whores are like American businessmen away from home: a few drinks and out come the snapshots of the kids. I have learned to coo admiringly and can say "What nice eyes" in several languages, usually a safe comment no matter what the child looks like. I met a disarming member of the profession in 1960 on the overnight boat from Tenerife to Las Palmas in the Canary Islands. I was unable to get a cabin alone and my room-mate turned out to be a sprightly, talkative blonde who was delighted when she discovered I spoke Spanish. She brought out a bottle of Fundador and spent half the night telling me the problems of life as what is euphemistically called a B-girl in a Las Palmas waterfront bar-and-brothel. She had been to Tenerife to visit her seven-year-old daughter who was living with a family there. "I can't keep her with me," she said, adding primly, "It wouldn't be correct." She showed me a tinted photograph of the child in full First Communion regalia.

In the morning she helped me carry my bags off the boat and, as we shook hands, she invited me to drop in sometime and have a drink with her at the establishment where she worked. So I did. I had found a furnished apartment but it wasn't going to be ready for a couple of weeks and I was stuck in a rather dreary hotel. I didn't know anyone in town and I was bored stiff. It wasn't customary then for a woman to go drinking alone in bars or night-clubs of a Spanish city, so I decided to look up my shipmate. The place consisted of a large room with a long bar, a few tables and chairs, a jukebox, and the usual Rooms Upstairs. The patrons were mostly merchant seamen of different nationalities. "Sometimes they get beaten up and robbed," my friend confided, "and it makes me feel bad because I think, 'How would I like it if this happened to my own brother?'" She led me to a table in a corner and introduced me to the owner, a fat, affable, bedizened madam ("She's been like a mother to me"), who invited me to sit down and have a drink. A few co-workers were asked to join us. They all knew about me. "This is the American lady writer I met on the boat," she would say proudly to each one. I felt like the guest of honor at a women's club tea.

After an hour of polite chitchat, she got permission in honor of the occasion to take the rest of the night off. Together with one of the other girls, a Tunisian with frizzy black hair and enormous dark eyes, she took me on a tour of the Las Palmas waterfront. The only drawback was that at every place they formally introduced me to the owner or manager, who escorted us into a private back room or the kitchen or, in one place, a sort of storeroom with a large box we used for a table. There we would sit and drink sedately with a few privileged characters who were selected to meet me. They asked me endless questions, mostly about America. From out front I could hear the jukebox music, the laughter, the noises of a crowded bar. "Why can't we stay out there?" I would ask hopefully, but they would shake their heads emphatically. "Oh no! It's not a nice place for a lady. Too many rough characters." If, on our passage through to backroom privacy, a bar customer tried to speak to me, my protectors angrily warned him off, and if anyone used profane language in front of me they would shush him quickly. I began to understand how a head of state feels, frustratingly surrounded by aides and bodyguards, and I had a wild desire to break through the barrier and start shaking hands, but I didn't want to upset my guardians.

When the bars closed we went to a house of assignation in the countryside for more drinks and something to eat. By this time we had been joined by a very black Liberian girl, a Spanish girl from Barcelona and two rather taciturn Canary Island males, understandably puzzled by my presence. They all took me in a taxi back to my hotel around six in the morning. They hadn't let me spend a cent all night, even to buy a round of drinks, although I repeatedly offered. "No, no," they would say. "You are our guest." It was an oddly innocent and pleasant outing.

Years ago, I did a lot of whorehouse drinking in Havana. Nowadays, in the new Cuba, prostitution has been eliminated under the puritanical Castro regime through a process of vocational retraining. No more sitting around in the old kimona. Instead, the girls were sent to cut sugar cane or taught how to operate sewing machines or drafted into some similarly productive occupation. In the beginning of the transformation I sometimes wondered how all those amiable Cuban strumpets, frisky as kittens, took to the rehabilitation process. At least one of them I met left for the

United States. I remember her because her stunning speciality was to smoke a cigarette with her vagina. On the one occasion I witnessed this, I watched dumbfounded with envy of her astonishing muscular dexterity as she steadily inhaled, making the tip of the cigarette glow red, and blew out smoke, never removing the cigarette until it was only a butt. Like her sister professionals she was easily shocked by departure from what she considered proper protocol and volubly denounced any impropriety of language as insulting to her status as an *artista*.

Two other examples that come to mind occurred while I was living in Havana. I was drinking with Kendrigan and two other people in a nightclub when a visiting executive of an American broadcasting company came over to our table. Kendrigan had met him earlier in the day and he introduced him. The man asked if he could join us. He seemed like any other normally boring American businessman until he asked me to dance. As I was trying to follow his inept version of the rumba, he murmured in my ear, "I want to eat your shit." I thought I surely must have misunderstood. "Pardon?" He repeated it. I suppose I should have staggered back aghast and hissed, "Sir, how dare you?" However, I am no Samuel Richardson heroine carrying smelling salts in my reticule in case of shock. I don't faint at an insult and I don't make scenes. I was certainly surprised but I couldn't think of an appropriate response. Who could? ("Be my guest" . . . "Sorry, but I'm constipated" . . . "Wouldn't you settle for a good steak?") I simply led him back to our table, where I had a double tequila and ignored him.

A little later, two other American men, acquaintances of my coprophilic dance partner, also sat down with us. When the club showed signs of closing, they insisted that we take them to a brothel. Once there, my friends and I were drinking and paying no attention to the proceedings, but the three tourists were intently watching a circus. Suddenly, with no warning, the broadcasting executive pulled off all his clothes, threw himself face downward on the bed and began bouncing up and down, yelling, "I want a prick in my cunt." The startled whores recoiled in disgust. "Take this dreadful creature out of here immediately!" they demanded. They kept expostulating indignantly as his friends managed to get him dressed and bundled him into a taxi while my friends and I drove off in our car with me thinking, "You never know what people are really like," and with Kendrigan saying sorrowfully, "I'll never be able to show my face in that house again. Cuban whores won't stand for that sort of performance. They're very correct, you know."

The second incident happened in another brothel to which I took an American journalist after a night of drinking around town. I thought we were just going for more booze, according to my custom as a dedicated all-night drinker, but as we were chatting with the girls, everyone fully dressed, the inebriated writer stood up, unzipped his fly, revealing an impressive erection, and asked, "Which one of you girls is going to suck my prick?" The whores were horrified. As he advanced toward them, waving his weapon, they scampered to the other side of the room. Obviously, he was getting no volunteers. They huddled together, scowling at him. "How can you be so crude in front of the lady?" one demanded disapprovingly, while another commented, looking sympathetically at me, "*Qué paciencia tiene la señora!*" They urged me to take him home to sober him up and they helped me get him into a taxi, with me apologizing for his behavior. The next day I said to him, "Well, you certainly made a spectacle of yourself last night." "What do you mean?" "I mean that people I know go to whorehouses to drink. They don't go to *do* anything." "I do," he said.

I suppose the worst place I've been in, the nadir of rock-bottom cut-throat dives, was a dancehall-cum-brothel about an hour's drive from Mexico City. I was taken there late one night in 1963 by a Mexican film director and actor, a huge, flamboyant man. During the long drive I had to pee. "I know just the place," he said. We stopped at a dark building in front of which stood an armed policeman. My escort explained my problem and the policeman led me into a large room where in the dim light I could barely make out rows of cots filled with recumbent forms. At the back was one of the worst toilets I've ever seen. When I came out, I thanked the policeman. "*Muchas gracias. Es muy amable.*" (Literally, this means, "You are very lovable," but it's a common way of saying, "You are very kind.") As we drove off, I asked, "What in God's name was that place?" "It's a women's prison," he said.

Just before we reached our destination I handed him all my money, insisting that he take it, as I was on an expense account, doing a magazine survey of the arts in Mexico, and he had been helping me. When we had been in the place an hour or so, after dozens of tequilas, it became increasingly evident that my escort was roaring drunk. He began insulting the bedraggled "hostess" he himself had invited to sit with us. I apologized to her, at the same time reprimanding him sharply. He glared at me fiercely, got up and strode from the room in a huff. It was not until a half hour later that we realized he had taken his car and driven off, leaving me stranded miles out in the country. He had been ordering drinks for all and sundry, but he departed without paying the bill and with every cent I had with me. The whores were clucking in dismay. "What a horrible thing for him to do!" . . . "*Qué bruto!*" . . . "The scoundrel!"

It didn't occur to me to be frightened, although I guess I should have been. (The husband of Ruth Coronel, Diego Rivera's daughter, said to me some days later, when I told him where I had been, "But no one *ever* goes there. You were lucky to get out alive.") I sat at the table, surrounded by chattering men and women. They looked like what they were: old, beat-up, last-ditch whores, the dregs, while the men—pimps, waiters, customers, whatever—were evil-eyed, scar-faced thugs. They were a terrible-looking bunch, but they couldn't have been kinder to me or more sympathetic. "We might as well all have another drink," the manager said. Finally, I thought of a solution. "Look," I said. "If you can get me back to my hotel in Mexico City, I have some travelers' cheques there and I will pay the bill." Two of the men and four whores and I piled into a dilapidated car and off we set, arriving at the entrance of the fashionable María Isabel Hotel shortly before 9 A.M. The doorman looked astounded, as well he might. When I started to get out, I overheard one of the men say to one of the old bags, "You better go with her and make sure she gets the money." "No," she said. "She's all right. We can trust her."

The hotel cashier's office was open when I came down from my room and I cashed a cheque and then returned to my waiting group, sitting outside in the sunlight, looking like something out of a late-night horror movie. I paid the bill and then invited them all for breakfast. They suggested the Xochimilco Floating Gardens and soon I found myself in a boat, where the whores hovered over me in motherly fashion, wrapping a serape around me to protect me from the breeze and insisting that I eat. They had loaded the boat with food and flowers and they hired a mariachi band to accompany us in another boat, singing and playing. I enjoyed every minute. "How fortunate that you were left with us," the whores kept saying. "You could have been left with bad people. It could have been very dangerous for you." They were right. Also, they refused to take any more money from me or to let me pay for our breakfast fiesta. "You paid the bill for our place," they said. "Now this is our treat."

Some years earlier, in 1957, I had a much more perilous experience in another Mexican brothel where I narrowly missed getting shot. I had been to a press showing of a tourist bureau film, followed by a cocktail party that lasted way into the evening. The vice-president of an advertising company was delegated to escort me back to my hotel. Instead, we visited a number of bars and when everything was closed, even the roisterous resort called Tenampa, we headed for La Casa de La Bandida, a famous brothel. We sat drinking in the parlor with a whore, her pimp and two customers—a newspaperman, I think, and a rugged, blue-eyed Mexican who was some sort of road construction superintendent in a wild country region. He carried a .45 gun which, for the time being, he had removed from its holster and left on the parlor table. I was drinking tequila, and a barefooted maid with two long, thick braids of ink-black hair kept bringing me fresh bottles. Everyone except me and my escort, whom I'll call Manolo because that was his name, was snorting cocaine. They offered us some but we refused. "I never touch anything but pot," I said, at which the pimp disappeared for a half hour and returned with a joint. I thought it would be impolite to refuse, after he'd gone to the trouble of getting it, but it was the strongest I've ever smoked. Between that and the tequila, I was in high gear. I had an engagement to interview Ava Gardner at noon, an appointment I'd spent a week trying to get but which now seemed irrelevant. I asked the pimp to telephone the film press agent and cancel. "Dígale que lo siento que no puedo cumplir con la compromesa porque estoy fumando mota en una casa de putería," I said gaily.

("Tell him that I'm sorry I can't keep the appointment because I'm smoking pot in a whorehouse.")

The whore had been sullen and withdrawn at first but I finally won her over. She told me she came from Yucatán, where she used to work in a factory and where her two children—out came the snapshots—were living with her parents. She also said bitterly that she hated every man she went with, which was the first time I had heard that from any prostitute. (In fact, none of them ever talked to me about their work and I never asked them.) The cocaine really hit her and when another patron joined us in the parlor, she soon had him lying on his back in a corner of the room, with her astride, riding up and down. I was sitting on a sofa with the pimp beside me. We were having a spirited discussion about Mexican politics. "Look at me! See what I'm doing," she called to him, trying to attract his attention. "Don't bother me," he said. "Can't you see I'm talking to the lady?" At that, she sprang from the man, leaving him literally up in the air, grabbed the .45 from the table and fired two shots, bang bang, at the pimp. If he hadn't instinctively dropped to the floor like a flash, he probably would have been dead, as one bullet went into the sofa back, right where he had been sitting. The second bullet lodged in the wall above the sofa, two inches from my head. I was too paralyzed to move. The blue-eyed man grabbed the gun from her hand but she seized a bottle, broke it on the tile floor and started toward the pimp, just as four tough-looking goons rushed into the room, grabbed her by the arms and legs, spread-eagled, and dragged her out. I stood up, shouting, "Do not treat her in that manner!" She called out to me, "You are not to blame. But remember what I told you. I meant every word I said. I hate them all."

The rest of us had sobered up with remarkable speed, and Manolo and I left. It was then late afternoon. As we started to get into his car, two of the goons appeared threateningly at our side. "You were treated all right, weren't you?" they said. "You have no complaints, have you?" Their look and manner were chilling, and I was far more scared than I had been inside. The blue-eyed man, who had come out with us, quickly stepped between us and the goons. "Get in the car and leave," he said quietly. "I'll handle this." We hightailed away, considerably subdued. I realized that if I had been shot it would have been in all the papers. It would have been if any tourist were shot in such circumstances, but I could just imagine the heading: "Author of Latins Are Lousy Lovers Shot in Whorehouse." Everyone would have thought I was not only some kind of sex pervert but a dope fiend, to boot.

The episode had a curiously happy sequel. The first Christmas after my husband died, I took my two children to Acapulco for what would have been too mournful a holiday had we stayed home. We stopped a week in Mexico City and ran into Manolo, who invited us to his home for a family dinner. It turned out he had told his wife about our risky night out, just as I had told my husband. They both knew that we had been guilty of nothing more than extreme foolhardiness, although Jack said, "It's a fine thing! I'm home here, taking care of the children, cooking hamburgers every night, and you're getting shot at in a Mexican whorehouse." But he, too, was a whorehouse drinker and he understood.

The dinner was a warmhearted, sentimental Latin affair with Manolo and his wife, their two children, a grandmother, myself, my children, all one happy family. Manolo proposed a toast to the memory of my husband; I proposed one to Mrs. Manolo; we drank to our children; we drank to each other. "This woman and I faced death together," Manolo announced dramatically, for all the world as if he and I had fought side by side on the barricades. We drank to that, too, and the grandmother got up and ran around the table, kissing everyone in turn. After dinner their teen-age daughter and my teen-age daughter each played the piano while our small sons set off fireworks on the patio. The next day I sent flowers, and for several years we exchanged Christmas cards. For what could have been a lethal episode in disreputable circumstances, it was a curiously homey ending.

*   *   *

All that was a generation or so ago, while my Vassar excursion into Albany's red-light district was over fifty years ago. My last visit to such an establishment was in 1965 in Madrid, a place I heard about from Sir Alec Guinness. I hasten to say that it was by no means a personal recommendation. Someone in the *Doctor Zhivago* film company had been talking about it and Guinness repeated the information.

Throughout the years I suppose I've probably been in more whorehouses, just drinking and talking, neither client nor inmate, than any other woman. I hope I haven't sounded patronizing, because that's not the way I felt. I think I must have regarded it all somewhat the way I did speakeasies. The Volstead Act—the 18th Amendment to the Constitution, known as Prohibition—went into effect in 1920 after it had been passed by Congress, vetoed by Woodrow Wilson and then passed again, over his veto. I did my first drinking in December 1923, and Repeal wasn't until December, 1933. I don't mean that during that decade I drank steadily. What I mean is that my initiation into social drinking took place in an atmosphere of the illicit, an atmosphere that persisted for ten years. The speakeasy attraction was not that we were all crazy for drink but that we were venturing into a fascinating area of the forbidden. I was never an alcoholic and could take it or leave it, although I usually took it. It was part of the pattern of my generation.

Things are different today. Oh, I suppose one could still get a drink in a whorehouse, but I doubt if people go to such places in the style of the Thirties. As I said earlier, it used to be fashionable to visit a brothel and pay money to watch a lesbian performance. Nowadays, from what I hear and read, you just stay home and invite your friends over. Do-it-yourself daisy chains.

The whores are today getting organized into trade unions (when they aren't busy writing best sellers), as well they need to be, with all the amateur competition. The Pill and the sexual revolution have wrought havoc with job security for professionals. Nevertheless, I think it doubtful if the oldest profession will soon become obsolete like other once thriving businesses based on demand—purveyors of whalebone for ladies' corsets, or buttonhook manufacturers, for instance—mostly because of certain practical reasons but also because there still clings to the harlot a remnant of that legendary lure of sinful enticement. There's something else, too. "Why do you like whores?" I asked a Mexican friend. He would never take me to a brothel for drinks, although I knew he occasionally went, and not just for drinks. He was extremely attractive to women and easily had his pick, for free —society beauties, Hollywood stars, visiting tourists. All women found him charming and irresistible. But when I asked him the question, he answered, "They're exciting. They know how to make a man happy. They always act glad to see you but if you don't go back for a time they never ask, 'Where have you been? Why haven't you come to see me?' They're always good-natured with a man. No tears, no temper, no demands, no strings, none of the problems of an affair. Just pleasure." I think he had a point.

> First you ring the bell and ask for Anna.
> Then you put a nickel in the player piano.
> Down comes the madam and says, "Well, dearie,
> Want to buy a drink just to make us cheery?"
> Down comes Anna in the red kimona,
> All smelled up with perfume and cologne-a.
> You sit in the parlor, feeling all prime,
> Then you spend $2 for a real good time.
>
>   Folk song of the Twenties

Chapter Two

HOW NOW, FELLATIO!

I have long been puzzled by language taboos. Many people today profess to be horrified, and probably are, by the relaxation of the ban on words they call "obscene," but I could never understand why it was considered all right to say or write one word while another word meaning the same thing and bringing to mind exactly the same image was forbidden. In 1925 I wrote a term paper at Vassar in which I expressed this puzzlement. Why was it acceptable, I asked, to use make love, sleep with, copulate or any of the dozens of other euphemisms, but unthinkable to use fuck? Words, I argued, are only sounds: combinations of vowels and consonants. Why should some be considered proper and others shocking? It is not because the sound itself is ugly. People don't recoil at luck, pluck, truck, buck. No one shudders at the sound of punt or runt. It is not the meaning, either, because, as I just said, a synonym is permissible. It is not because of the snobbish assumption that the forbidden word is used by social outcasts or the lower classes. On the contrary. I learned the words at Vassar. Today they're more or less in general usage, perhaps even by whores. This fashionable trend began as an upper middle class manifestation of the chic, the hip—at least in the case of girls—and then gradually percolated downward in society. A few years ago, Philip Zimbardo, a Stanford psychologist, was quoted on the subject as saying, "Lower class women don't curse, at least before

men." Nor do lower class men curse in front of women. Michael
Caine, the actor, told me that the famous Cockney rhyming
slang was invented because "Cockneys don't use bad language in
front of women. They may if they're angry, but not in conversation."

For those who don't know, in Cockney slang one speaks the
first of two associated words. The unspoken second word rhymes
with the taboo word one means. Thus, Khyber means ass because
of Khyber Pass, and cobblers means balls, because of cobblers'
awls. This reluctance to "talk dirty" in front of their womenfolk
was, and in some cases still is, common to working-class men of all
nations. During the many years I was involved with the labor
movement on the New York waterfront, I found that if a seaman
or longshoreman even said son of a bitch in front of me, he would
quickly excuse himself. ("Pardon my French.") In fact, my own
language was so much more uninhibited that my seaman husband
once complained, "You're turning our home into a fo'c's'le."

Years ago the so-called four-letter words were banned in print.
Frank Crowninshield, editor of Vanity Fair, used to tell a story
about Mr. Scribner, head of the publishing house. According to
Crowny, Mr. Scribner once insisted to Hemingway that the
latter must delete one word from a book Scribner's was going to
publish. When Hemingway asked what the word was, Mr. Scribner could not bring himself to utter it. Instead, he wrote it on his
daily engagement pad and pushed it over so the writer could see
it. When the two went out to lunch, Mr. Scribner's secretary was
somewhat surprised, when straightening his desk, to note that on
his pad for that day's appointments, after various engagements for
the day, her boss had written "Fuck."

Many of us remember the furore over some of the language in
James Jones's From Here to Eternity. Now, it all seems stupid to
have made a fuss, and it was stupid at the time, especially when
anyone could go to a library and read Chaucer, Shakespeare, Pie-
tro Aretino, Rabelais, Ovid and dozens of other classics all using
forbidden words. At the time of the Earl of Longford's crusade
against pornography and obscenity in England a few years ago,
one Lord Platt asked ironically, during a sulphurous Parliament
debate, what they, the would-be reformers, intended to do about
the Bible. He said the Old Testament contained "some of the

most lewd, crude and obscene chapters" he had read anywhere in literature. He added that he would not complain that this obscene book was on sale, save for the fact that it was "sold in the children's departments of bookshops, is in school libraries, in the windows of the Mothers' Union, and is given away as school prizes."

In the preceding chapter I couldn't have written the word whore in former days. I would have had to substitute harlot, scarlet woman, tart, or possibly, in some cases, prostitute. Whorehouse would have become a house of ill repute or a house of ill fame. Yet they all mean the same. What's the difference? Some years ago, many newspapers refused to accept advertisements for a production of Ford's seventeenth-century Jacobean classic shocker *'Tis Pity She's a Whore*, without deleting the last word, thus printing the title as *'Tis Pity She's a. . . .* This kind of ridiculous hypocrisy has not entirely vanished. A frequent example is the use by some publications of "f---." This is ludicrous. The sight of the full word spelled out is not going to make any of the readers keel over in a dead faint.

True, the situation has improved since the early days of my childhood, when underwear was called unmentionables, legs were limbs, and genitals were private parts. (In Evelyn Waugh's diary there is a quote from a girl who was one of London's Bright Young Things in the Twenties: "I don't see why they call them private parts. Mine aren't private.") I never heard either of my parents even say damn, while my grandmother's strongest expletives were "Rats!" and "Fiddlesticks!" When I was at boarding school a menstrual period, when not called the curse, as it still is, was referred to as "I fell off the roof" or "my cousin from Harvard." One never went to the toilet. It was always "I have to powder my nose" or "I have to see a man about a dog." These priggish evasions have been discarded by today's forthright young, although many of their elders still cling to them under the delusion that they are being "refined." The British consider it more refined to say lavatory. To say toilet is lower class. (Another of Frank Crowninshield's favorite stories was about a posh party at which the butler announced the guests. When one elegant lady arrived and murmured "Lady Lavery," the butler leaned toward her and said in a discreet tone, "Down that hall, madam, first door on the left.") It takes someone with an impeccably upper class background like David Niven to say casually, as he did when he first met me in the bar of London's Connaught Hotel, "I've got to piss." Or the Duke of Bedford. Not that he said piss, but I bet he wouldn't be caught dead saying lavatory. When I went to Woburn Abbey to interview him, the first thing he said to me after hello was "Would you like to use the bathroom?" As it so happened, I'd been dashing wildly around the grounds trying to find one, finally locating a public one in the nick of time. I told him about it, complaining that there was no mirror. He immediately took out a pad and pencil from his pocket and made a note: "No mirror in women's toilet." (He also told me, "I'd rather cut my throat than lift my drink and say 'Cheers.'" I loved him for that.)

In Britain, to a far greater extent than in America, language is not only a matter of age groups but of caste. Young people use the taboo words, but the only older people who do so are those of the upper classes, especially the more intellectual ones. The first newspaper ever to print "fuck" was a London one, either *The Times* or *The Observer*, I forget which. The occasion was an attempt about fifteen years ago to prevent the sale of *Lady Chatterly's Lover*, on charges of obscenity. The paper was reporting the trial proceedings. It quoted the testimony of a witness for the defense who explained to the court that one of the words to which the prosecution objected vehemently was a legitimate part of the English language. "It is," he said, "a verb: to fuck. As in, I fuck, you fuck, he fucks." The paper printed his words with no apology, no comment, no missing letters. Thus a blow was struck for common sense.

At the time of this trial, all the newspapers published scores of letters from readers, many of them asking indignantly, "Would you want your wife [sister, mother, daughter] to read this book?" Commenting on these letters, one correspondent wrote, "The only appropriate question is, 'Would you want your gamekeeper to read this book?'"

It was an Englishman, too, who first uttered the word on television. After this historic first by Kenneth Tynan, the word has been heard on British TV from time to time, usually in documentaries or TV film coverage of news events. One interview with an American professor at Berkeley in California, during the early student riots, did not censor the professor when he described how he was confronted by an angry student who shouted at him, "You bourgeois Jewish motherfucker!" The professor said that although startled, he had replied, "You are correct in some aspects but not in all."

Such truthful coverage would be impossible on American television, which bleeps out even milder expletives common to most of us. Of course, British TV and radio stations receive telephone calls and letters from affronted viewers and listeners but, to their credit, they usually ignore them, although the BBC did apologize to their audience when Peregrine Worsthorne, a well-known conservative journalist, appeared on a program to discuss the sex scandal involving government figures Lords Jellico and Lambton. When asked what effect it had on the British public, Worsthorne replied, to the consternation of his interlocutor, "I don't think they give a fuck."

There was a time, not too long ago, when "bloody" was about the worst thing one could say in Britain. Its use was horrifying, unthinkable in print or in front of ladies. To us in America, this was incomprehensible. Therein lies one of the silliest aspects of language taboos. What is acceptable in one country is considered obscene or outrageous in another. Although bloody is now used in England even by respectable old ladies, its use is banned in radio interviews. On the other hand, "Keep your pecker up" is a common phrase meaning "keep a stiff upper lip," not, as we would think, an admonishment to keep your penis erect. Similarly, when a Britisher says, "I knocked her up," he does not mean he got a girl pregnant. He means that he woke her up. The word "knickers" is still considered faintly naughty and is always good for audience hilarity when uttered by a comedian, even though it is in common usage, as I discovered when I went to a London doctor for a check-up. "Take off everything except your knickers," he said. To me, knickers were knickerbockers, or plus fours, as worn in my youth by men playing golf or by boys. "Except my *what?*" I asked. The doctor repeated it, and I realized he meant my underpants.

In France one of the most obscene insults used to be, and perhaps still is, to call someone *cochon*, pig. In Spanish-speaking countries, the same is true of *cabrón*, goat. All through Latin America words that are polite to say in one country are often considered obscene in another. Thus, in Cuba one does not order papaya because that is slang for cunt. Instead, one says *fruta bomba*. And so it goes, making the whole business of "dirty" words a farce. Everyone knows that excrement means shit. The latter is now common, both in print and in speech, but there was a time when it was inadmissible, although excrement and ordure were both usable, and if one said *merde* it was okay because even if the meaning was known, it sounded all right in French— to an American, that is—just as faeces, provided one could pronounce it, was acceptable because it is Latin. Isn't it all ridiculous?

There is one word that is still, permissive age or not, pretty much on the blacklist. That word is cocksucker, although back in the Thirties my friends and I sometimes used this supposedly inelegant but certainly explicit term. More common expressions were "to French," to "go down on," or, in the homosexual world, to "do someone for trade." A blow job is of recent vintage. As for fellatio, we never even heard of it or saw it in print. It is only recently that I learned how to pronounce it. To me, it sounds like a character in Italian opera or Shakespeare. "How now, Fellatio. Why dost thou tarry?"

As a child, right after World War I, I once heard some men singing the doughboys' ditty, *Mademoiselle from Armentières*, of which one couplet struck me as a complete puzzle; "the French they are a peculiar race, They fight with their feet and they fuck with their face, hinky dinky parlez-vous." It might as well have been Sanskrit but the lines stuck in my memory. I never asked anyone what they meant and it was a long time before I found out.

During my stint as a newspaper reporter in Syracuse, New York, during the Twenties, I gained a vague idea that the practice of Frenching, or whatever it was called, was something degraded, indulged in by perverts and so out of the ordinary that prostitutes charged extra for it. I had only the sketchiest notion of what it entailed. Although I had several affairs during those years, no one ever suggested that I perform the act, even though three of my more devoted suitors made oral love to me. I had never even heard of this practice, and the first time it happened to me I was absolutely astounded. I thought the man had gone mad, like whatshisname—was it Nebuchadnezzar?—who got down on the ground and ate grass. However, I learned to accept it as an expression of love for my body and a desire to give me pleasure. It never entered my head that I might be expected to reciprocate, nor, I believe, did it occur to the men. If it did, there was no sign. My first fellatio experience was in 1931. My German husband and I were in the guest room, called the spare room, of my grandmother's house in LaFargeville. I was lying on my back with him kneeling over me when suddenly, with no warning, he thrust his erect penis into my mouth. I thought it was going straight down my throat and I was in utter panic, as well as gagging. I was also conscious of how grotesque I must look. Whatever else can be said about sex, it cannot be called a dignified performance. I lay there paralyzed, my eyes shut tight and, of course, unable to speak. Finally, I managed to wriggle out from under, scurried into the bathroom and threw up. It was definitely an unromantic initiation. I was embarrassed, but most of all I felt a perfect idiot. What on earth was I supposed to do with the thing? It isn't something that happens instinctively. It's an acquired taste, like oysters.

My next contact with what used to be called an "unnatural practice" (as in lurid hints like "He forced her to perform an unnatural act") was not personal. It happened to a friend—let's call her Maeve—a tall, slender young blonde who worked on one of the Condé Nast magazines. She met George Jean Nathan at an office party and he asked her out for dinner. Afterward, they went back for more drinks to his apartment in the Hotel Royalton. The next day she confided in me and Tina, another Nast employee. Nathan, America's greatest drama critic, was one of our literary idols and we were thrilled that one of us had actually had a date with him. Our reverent illusions were shattered when Maeve described what took place. "We had drinks, sitting on the sofa, with him edging nearer. I was willing to lay him. After all, he's the great George Jean Nathan. But I certainly thought he'd be a little smoother at it. The first thing he said was, 'Thank God you're tight!' which seemed pretty crude, I thought. Then something happened to him. He kept banging away and I just lay there, wondering if he was ever going to finish. Apparently not. He sat up and said, "Take it in your mouth, darling. It'll stiffen right up.' We were surrounded by pictures of Lillian Gish staring down at us from the table, the desk, the walls. I suddenly thought the whole business was a ghastly mistake. I got out of there as fast as I could."

We were really shocked by this tale and whenever we saw Nathan after that, we glared at him. What a terrible experience for poor Maeve, we thought.

Nevertheless, our little group gradually began to realize that this practice was evidently something men found especially pleasurable and that any woman who wanted to be considered good in bed had better know how to do it. A few of us decided we would simply have to learn. But how? Back in those days we had no Linda Lovelace-type movies to show us the technique, no specific instruction books or manuals, no magazine columns of helpful advice. I had a homosexual friend and I told him our dilemma and asked for practical hints on procedure. After he finished laughing, he outlined some primary-grade instructions, which I imparted to my best friend, Meg, during a lunch at Schrafft's. "Jim says," I began, seizing the salt cellar, "you take it like this," and I went on, earnestly repeating his instructions, with Meg listening incredulously, interpolating occasional questions—"But then what do you do?"—until we both became aware that the women at the next table were listening, mesmerized to the point of forgetting their fudge sundaes.

I still have a letter I wrote to my old Vassar classmate, Amy, then living in Chicago. (She saved my letters and returned them to me years ago.) It is dated August 24, 1933, and gives a rough idea of our predicament. She had apparently written me about the problem because my letter, in which I have changed the names, reads as follows:

"As to cocksucking, you really should come to New York and join our class. Meg and Tina and I have all decided we want to learn how. So we are practicing like mad, every chance we get, and we are all of us simply lousy at it. I think it is really pathetic. We are such nice girls and we have such an innocent, worthwhile attitude toward it, really wonderful spirit, but we just don't seem to be any good, no matter how hard we try. We ask everybody we can about it and then rush to have lunch together and impart the new information. We each keep practicing in a dogged way, although it is getting pretty hard to get any men to practice on, we are so terrible. Then we meet again to compare notes and seriously discuss the different techniques. I asked Freddie because he is a captain in the merchant marine and has known girls all over the world. He said we ought to practice on a banana, the idea being not to leave any teeth marks on it. He also had another tip, but we think it's too ridiculous. He said if we don't seem to be making any headway, we should run to the bathroom, rinse our mouths with water as hot as we can stand, and then race back again. Said it works like magic. We all think we feel foolish enough as it is, without going through any such rigamarole. Besides, in my apartment it takes ages for the water to get hot. . . . Anyway, I did it with that young British scientist I wrote you about. Not the hot water, just the regular cocksucking, and I'm telling you, Amy, it took me a half hour at the very least, and I kept thinking, 'If this goes on for another single second, I shall *die!*' Then, after I finally got through, he confided that he really doesn't care much for that sort of thing. You would think that would be enough to discourage me forever, but no. I tried again with Freddie but had to stop. Either stop or else choke to death. Jim says I've been doing it all wrong, so he described a new method and I promptly told Meg and Tina. Meg tried it and says there's nothing in it. She was about ready to give up. She says she keeps trying and trying and all she ever gets is sick. She says she doesn't know whether to keep grinding away at it and get her degree or give it all up and be a sexual flop. She told us she was going away at it one night and all of a sudden she said "Oh HELL!" and gave up, and both she and her lover got to laughing till they almost fell off the bed. She said to him, 'Do you think I'll ever be any good at it?' and he said, 'No!' He says the trouble with all of us is that we're too businesslike about it, that we are serious about wanting to learn and we go about it as if we were learning our Latin verbs, methodically, like little ants, determined to win out if it kills us. (I know ants don't learn Latin but never mind. You get what he means.) He said that is just the trouble, that we lack oompah and that none of us really likes it and that he will be damned if he's going to let Meg practice on him any more because he might want to use it for something else some day. Tina, of course, has an awful time because of her protruding buck teeth. Jim says she hasn't got a Chinaman's chance of ever being a really A-Number One cocksucker, but he says I should make a good one. But I think I am probably the worst of the lot. The last time I tried it, Freddie *fell asleep* while I was doing it! Besides, my long hair is always getting in the way. I can't go to bed with it pinned on top of my head like a washerwoman. Also, I have no one to practice on most of the time, as my British scientist is at Yale on a Rockefeller Fellowship and only comes to New York on occasional weekends, and Freddie is away at sea a lot. Tina has Charlie and she makes him let her try it every time she sees him, willy nilly, and he just has to suffer, although the last time she really thought she was getting somewhere because after she had been at it for some time he began to groan and grunt, but then he sat up and began to scratch his foot and said it had been itching him and he couldn't stand it any longer. So Tina began to cry and said she had never been so humiliated in her entire life and she would never, never try again."

In spite of our problems, we kept gritting our teeth, determined to persevere, hating it, but spurred on by stubborn ambition to succeed. Pikes Peak or bust.

Curiously, I've never known any Latin man—Cuban, Mexican, Venezuelan, Spanish, Italian—who wanted me to do it, or who would even let me do it the one or two times I made a gesture in that direction. I thought at the time, and I still think, that it was because they associated the act only with whores. However, maybe they just didn't think I'd be any good at it. They were wrong. I disliked it, but I kept at it until I made the team and won my letter.

Today, the matter is purely academic as far as I'm concerned, but from what younger women tell me, it's still no lead-pipe cinch for the beginner. I am assured that there are women who really enjoy it and can't wait to get at it. I accept this, but I myself have never known any woman who felt this way. The women I've known—and I include myself—made oral love to men, not for their own pleasure, but for that of the men. It was an unselfish act, because none of them liked it. As for that topsy-turvy tangle called *soixante-neuf*, personally I have always felt it maddeningly confusing—like trying to pat your head and rub your stomach at the same time.

Chapter Three

————— ◆ —————

I KNOW WHO I AM

I have toyed with the idea of calling this book a novel, writing it in the first person and telling the truth, but giving myself a fake name. If others are doing it, why don't I?

Of course, there's nothing new in writing about yourself and pretending it's fiction. Doris Lessing did it in *The Golden Notebook*, Simone de Beauvoir in *The Mandarins*, to take only two notable examples of modern times. Writers have always done this, but when it is done in the form of autobiography and then arbitrarily called a novel, I think it's a cop-out. You are writing about yourself but you don't want to come right out and admit, "This is me. I did and said these things" because you don't want to take the flack. Even if everyone suspects you've written about yourself, you can deny it.

Why should I? I'm not ashamed of my life or embarrassed by it. I may have to change some names to protect other people or to avoid possible libel. Libel is not necessarily falsehood. I don't write lies; I don't make things up; and I have an eidetic memory. However, the libel laws are curious, often comical. For instance, in the United States it is libelous to call anyone a Communist unless that person is dead or has openly admitted being a Communist, even though the Communist Party is legal.

In England the laws are even odder. When I had a book of personality profiles published there, the publisher's libel lawyer insisted that I could not quote the actor Lionel Stander, reminiscing about long ago Hollywood, as saying, "I could do better with broads than Robert Taylor." Why not? "Broad," the English lawyer solemnly informed me, "is American slang for prostitute, and Robert Taylor could sue." I told him he was wrong on both counts. Broad does not mean prostitute and Robert Taylor was dead. "Then his widow could sue." This was erroneous, but typical of the nit-picking indulged in by members of the profession. Oh well, I suppose it's a living. In *Stranger at the Party*, my first book of memoirs, the American publisher's lawyer required the deletion of the phrase that a former member of the National Maritime Union reminded me of an orangutan who had been taught how to talk. In a written commentary, the lawyer stated, "The author cannot refer to the gentleman as an orangutan unless she can prove it." I was zoologically wrong, anyway. He reminded me more of a gorilla.

So all right. I'll change names to save other people embarrassment, but I won't pretend that I'm not writing about myself. However, I refuse to indulge in too much fretful examination of my emotions. One quality that exasperates me in so many women writers today is their obsessive self-analysis. They interminably discuss what they call their identity crises or their search for identity. They keep trying to "find" themselves. They blether on, page after page, in attempts to answer the question that apparently worries them: "Who am I?" This seems to occupy a disproportionate part of their thought and time, in bed and out. They mull over their reactions to their sexual partners and vice versa, until I feel like saying, "Look, girls, why don't you relax and just lie back and enjoy it?"

Who am I? I never ask myself. I know who I am. I know myself. I know that, among other things, I am easygoing, good-natured, adaptable. I am also unaggressive, unambitious, prone to procrastination and the line of least resistance. I bow to no one as a dawdler, but it doesn't bother me. I can sit contentedly for hours, thinking idly or daydreaming. I can even just sit, my mind a blank. I also like to sleep, a bond I discovered I have with Yves Saint Laurent one day when I had lunch with him in his Paris home. Sleeping, we agreed, is not merely an escape or something we do when we're tired or because it is customary. It's a pleasure.

"I *love* sleeping," Yves said. "It's one of the things I most enjoy." I feel the same. Aside from rare occasions, I'm asleep soon after my head snuggles down on the pillow. I can sleep ten or more hours a night and then take a daytime nap. I don't feel I'm wasting time, because for me it's a gratifying practice, even a sensuous one, like a hot bath or lying lazily in the sun or savoring a delicious dessert, preferably one made of chocolate. This predilection for sleep is not the result of old age. I've always had it. I've been told that when I was a baby my nurse had to wake me in order to give me my morning bottle.

I have never had the faintest urge to visit a psychiatrist, but many of these women writers have done so. Indeed, at one period, almost everyone I knew—sane, middle-class, well-educated young men and women—either was in analysis or had been, instead of working out for themselves their comparatively piddling problems. They also insisted on boring their friends, who didn't even get paid for listening, by recounting much of what they had told the shrinks and what the shrinks said back. They were all trying to find out who they were. Their search was not only boring but, at times, silly. One woman I knew consulted her analyst each time before and after she had intercourse. She made sure that her lovers knew this, and then she wondered why they sometimes became impotent. I used to ponder what kind of psychiatrists these gullible people regarded with awe and accepted their pronouncements without question. The pretty wife of an old friend of mine explained to me that she had learned the reason women are afraid of mice, scream and climb on chairs at sight of them. It is, her analyst told her, because women think the mice will leap into their vaginas. I could only murmur that personally I'm not afraid of mice, that I think they're cute—I could never bear to set traps for them—and that if any creature wanted to leap into her vagina it was probably the psychiatrist.

She also told me that girls who take off their shoes at parties are sexually uninhibited. It seemed to me possible that girls take off their shoes because their feet hurt. Then, too, one night in the White Horse, a Greenwich Village tavern once the favorite haunt of Dylan Thomas, an intellectual young man in analysis of course —who wasn't?—expounded a theory almost as quaint as the one about mice. Women fear snakes, he had learned from his analyst,

because snakes represent penises. My comment was that I've
been afraid of snakes all my life but I've yet to see the penis I'm
afraid of.

You see, I went through this who-am-I and what is-life-all-about
stage when I was in my teens. Then I outgrew it.

For my seventh birthday a relative gave me a five-year diary
bound in elegant beige leather, my name embossed in gold letters.
Most of my entries were about my school marks, movies I saw,
books. For example, on February 19, 1918, when I was ten, I
listed books I had read recently. "*Pilgrims Progress:* A hard book
for children to understand. *Captains Courageous:* Pretty good,
though more for boys. *Anne of Green Gables* and *Rebecca of
Sunnybrooke Farm:* Clean. *David Harum:* A very interesting
book. Very humorous, very good. Thackeray's *Vanity Fair:* Pretty
good but I think maybe I am too young to appreciate it. Will
read again when I get older." When it came to *Ben Hur,* I went
all out and rambled on for nine pages, ending with a wild burst of
enthusiasm: "One of the most wonderful books ever written."

The summer I was fourteen I fell madly in love with an
Australian boy named Harold, also fourteen, who was visiting at
the cottage next to ours on the St. Lawrence River. We used to
hold hands during the once-weekly movies in the Methodist Tab-
ernacle; a few times he kissed me chastely on the lips; and we
would lie for hours gazing at each other, I in the hammock on my
porch, he in his hammock, separated by a luxuriant growth of
hydrangeas between the two cottages. When he left for New York
with his parents, I moped and cried for several days. Then I sat
down with my diary and, after bitter cogitation and more tears, I
wrote a manifesto of disillusionment, headed with his name and
the words, "I shall never marry and I dedicate this to you in memory of my first love." There followed a list of commandments for
my future guidance: "1. Put your trust in no man. 2. Never love
with your whole heart. 3. Keep a cool head amid all emotions and
reason, reason, reason! 4. Weigh everything in an unprejudiced
manner and always decide in the way most advantageous to yourself. 5. Control your emotions and yourself! 6. Use your mind,
your knowledge, your judgement. 7. Be cultured—travel, music,
art, literature, drama, history. 8. NEVER MARRY. 9. NEVER

FALL IN LOVE. 10. ENJOY YOURSELF BUT REMEMBER IT IS ONLY PLAY!!!"

I pinned these grim pages together and wrote on the outside page, "To be opened when I am 21." I never wrote in that diary again and I didn't even find it until a few years ago when I was going through an old trunk.

I started a new diary at boarding school and continued it at Vassar. Entries made when I was sixteen and seventeen are studded with remarks like, "Am reading Schopenhauer. He expresses so much that I think and feel! Am very depressed over the futility of everything. Life is so damn futile. I feel like Yank in *The Hairy Ape.* 'Christ! Where do I get off at?! Where do I fit in?'" I sedulously copied down pessimistic quotations ("Life swings like a pendulum backward and forward between pain and ennui"— Schopenhauer; "The world is a comedy for those who think, but a tragedy for those who feel"—Horace Walpole) and I avidly learned by heart such poetry of despair as Matthew Arnold's beautiful "Dover Beach," reciting to myself with particular relish those sonorous lines of the famous last verse, ". . . for the world, which seems/To lie before us like a land of dreams,/So various, so beautiful, so new,/Hath really neither joy, nor love, nor light,/Nor certitude, nor peace, nor help for pain;/And we are here as on a darkling plain/Swept with confused alarms of struggle and flight,/Where ignorant armies clash by night."

I thoroughly enjoyed anything that smacked of malism or doom. In fact, I was having a wonderful time going through the what-is-life-all-about stage. I liked studying, I was academically successful, I had good friends, I loved the theater, movies and, above all, books. I was never actually moody or a worrier. All of which made my preference for dire and gloomy exhortations even more sophomoric. Thank God I outgrew it. Not entirely, though. Not all at once. I soon became too busy earning a living to spend much time playing the what-is-life game, but all those books, all those quotations, went through a kind of filtering process in my mind. I took from them what I needed as a survival kit.

The adolescent pleasure of self-dramatization was a luxury in which I continued to indulge during my early twenties, although it was diluted by cynical self-knowledge, doubtless a hangover from my who-am-I period. I think its last manifestation was an account I wrote of a weekend I spent with a newspaperman in New York at, of all places for a lovers' assignation, the Knights of Columbus Hotel. I was twenty-one. I wrote it for my own amusement and then packed it away with the youthful diaries, my college scrapbooks and a childhood notebook filled with jejune and highly derivative attempts at poetry. I include it here because it illustrates my early attitudes toward relationships with men before I at last found out what love really is.

The Martyr (April 1929)

The girl sat on the bed in the hotel room and felt sorry for herself. Three quarters of an hour, and he hadn't come back yet. "I've got to run over to the office, darling, and look in at the composing room. I'll be back in half an hour and then we'll have dinner." Half an hour! It's quarter to six now. What does he think I am? He can just plump me down in a hotel room and then I can sit there and wait till he feels like coming back to take me to dinner or make love to me or something. I am the humble kind that men can do things like that to. Meek and patient. Sit around and wait and speak when I'm spoken to. I'll take anything and like it.

She got up and walked to the window and looked out. The lights of Eighth Avenue blazed back at her. She felt she ought to feel something poetic and responsive about their insistent glitter, but she couldn't think of anything to feel, so she gave it up. Ah, it was not always thus. Once, the winged words flew from her heart. When she was a girl at school, she came to New York for weekends. She could make all sorts of phrases about the lights then. Walking alone up Broadway at night, it used to hit her all of a sudden as she passed the Corticelli kitten and the Wrigley robots at Times Square. The great barbaric glare of neon beauty. Oh city of dreadful light.

Now, she couldn't feel anything. Not a sparkle, not a glimmer. No fire struck from the flint. Dead, dead—and lost. In youth she had flung her banners wide and cried slogans to the stars. "It's just a phase," the elders said. And, tolerantly, "You'll outgrow it,

my dear." And she had thought, "But no, but no. They lie in
their teeth. I shall burn with it till the day on which I die.
Fiercely, fiercely, this flame I shall feed. On this heat I shall thrive
and flourish and from it wrench that quenchless power which car-
ries the secret of invulnerability."

But the elders had been right. The years had laid stale fingers
on her heart, and ecstasy, the lovely, the imperishable, was lost to
her forever. She turned from the window and the lights. He hasn't
come yet. There is no help in my heart for this humiliation. Yet
there is no anger. Nor even bitterness. I feel nothing within me.
The comfortable anesthesia of acceptance denies me all false
solace of emotion, but a sense of drama remains.

She could see herself deserted and forlorn. The quality of self-
pity was feigned but she must pamper it. She should be pacing up
and down the room, chain-smoking cigarettes, hot of heart and
sullen. Obedient to the demands of her fantasy, she lit a cigarette
and started to pace. Once around the room she went, and twice,
and three times. She looked at the pictures on the walls: the
Wallace Nutting rose garden in Maine, the imitation Corot land-
scape, the steel etching of the cathedral at Rheims. She remembered visiting the cathedral at Amiens, with the painting of Mary
and Martha taking the dead Christ from the cross, and how Els-
beth had said that it looked as if they were teaching Him to swim.
The memory made her laugh and disturbed her pose of militant
self-pity. After that, she got bored with her pacing and decided to
sit down again and brood. But she couldn't keep her mind on her
brooding. She tried to think of sad things, to keep her mind in the
proper mood. She pictured herself growing old and ugly, alone
and unloved and empty. She began to feel a little sad about that.
She thought of herself committing suicide. That would make everybody feel sorry for the way they had treated her. That would
show them. But she couldn't decide whether or not she would
leave a note, and if she did, whether it should be poetic and tender or gay and cynical. She became so interested in figuring out
what she would say that she forgot to be sad. So that was no
good.

She went back to her idea of pacing up and down the room and
smoking. In plays, nervous heroines always paced up and down,
inhaled smoke in deep drafts, tossed their heads back and blew it

out in streams through their nostrils, like fire-breathing dragons, and said "Oh God, oh God" over and over. She lit a cigarette and started to pace again. She inhaled the smoke, but not very far down, as it made her dizzy when she did that. She threw her head back and snorted smoke out through her nose, but some got in her eyes and made them water. She said "Oh God, oh God" but felt like a fool doing it. I am lousy at this, she thought.

She didn't want to smoke any more, as her throat felt sore. She looked at her watch. Half past six. I'm a fool to wait here, but why not? I haven't anything else to do. He wouldn't dare treat any other woman this way. I should be the queen type who demands attention and for whom men jump around and pick things up. A woman men wait on, instead of always insisting on doing everything for myself, rushing ahead and opening doors, leaping out of taxis without any help, scorning courtesy, always the prideless, but independent, role. I could work myself into a lather over this. I ought to, but there's some great lack in me. *The trouble is that I really don't care.* I really don't care about anything any more. What does it all matter? I am prideless and without honor. This is wrong, I guess, although I don't know just why, except that people are supposed to resent things and get "mad" when other people are mean to them. I never resent anything. Now I really must make myself feel something about this. I must work up a sense of injury.

But she couldn't feel anything, so she decided to take a nap, instead. She went over to the bed and curled up comfortably on it. My pillow should be wet with hot tears, she thought. So she felt very sad and wrinkled up her face and tried to cry. It was no use, and she forgot her martyrdom in sleep.

She awoke slowly, dimly conscious, half lost in that mystic, other world limbo of sleep. The air in the room was warm and stale. Suddenly becoming completely conscious, she jumped from the bed and turned on the light to look at her watch. Quarter of nine! My God, where *is* he? But she decided she couldn't really worry about it. She felt rested and peaceful. There is really no emotion in me at all, she thought. I suppose I'm lucky. I can storm around and cry and sulk, but it's always synthetic, always an act. Fundamentally, nothing can touch me. I never feel anything. If I ever do seem more sad and dramatic than usual, I can always trace it to the fact that I haven't had enough sleep or I've got a cold. Wasn't it in some psychology course that I learned that melancholy is often caused by a disturbance of the liver? I've got those melancholy liver blues.

She went in the bathroom and splashed cold water all over her face to take away the sleep traces. Then she powdered her nose and applied lipstick. An elevator door clattered in the hall and she heard Tom's footsteps. Oh dear, she thought, I suppose he's drunk or something, and here I've been having such a nice time all by myself.

She flew to the door. Then she stopped quickly and looked at the bed. She smiled as she went over to it and smoothed out the pillow and straightened the cover, carefully removing all evidence that it had been slept on. Then she opened the door. Tom stood there, looking very guilty. "Darling, I am so sorry," he said.

Instantly, something clicked within her. It was as if she were an actress who had been waiting in the wings and then found herself on the lighted stage, with the audience out front. She took her cue like a trouper. "Oh, you're sorry?" she said. "Well, so am I. I suppose you realize that I've been waiting here for you for four hours. I didn't know what to think. I didn't know what to do. I didn't know what might have happened to you."

"But darling, let me explain. . . ."

"There's no sense in your trying to explain. Wherever you were and whatever you were doing, you could have gotten to a telephone. You could have found some way to let me know. Here I was, pacing up and down the room, smoking one cigarette after another and crying my eyes out. You're the most inconsiderate man I've ever known. How did you think I was going to spend those four hours?"

"Why darling, you should have gotten some rest. Why didn't you take a nap? You said you were tired after the train."

"Take a nap! Take a *nap!*" Her voice rose to a scream and then broke. "And you can stand there and ask me why didn't I take a nap. This is the end. I've had enough." Tears filled her eyes and flowed down her cheeks into the corners of her mouth. Blindly, she pulled her cloche hat down over her eyes, clutched at her bag and started for the door. "Don't try to stop me. I'm through. You go out and leave me all alone for four hours and then you have

the nerve to tell me you thought I'd take a nap. God, I hate you."
She slammed the door.

Downstairs, on the street, she wiped away the tears and started
toward the subway. She passed the bright lights of a movie theater, passed them—and came back. She looked at the photographs
outside. She looked at her watch. Early yet, and this was a movie
she wanted to see. Of course, her heart was broken, but oh well
. . . She pushed her money through the little window. She was
still muttering to herself as she gave her ticket to the man at the
door and walked inside. "Take a nap, indeed!" she said.

Chapter Four

WHAT SEXUAL REVOLUTION?

Several times lately I have run into proponents of the quaint notion that back in the Thirties and Forties nice girls didn't sleep around. Nonsense. I didn't know anyone then who didn't have affairs. True, most of us didn't openly live with our lovers, as is now the custom, although many girls did. Our only objections to friends shacking up with men were not based on moral principles but concerned minor problems of etiquette, such as having to address Christmas cards to only one of the couple and then writing inside, "and to Bob, too," or how to introduce them—snags not always completely overcome today.

I never felt the slightest twinge of guilt about going to bed with a man I liked, and I'm sure none of my friends did, either, although a Yugoslav woman now living in London, a stunning beauty in her youth, recently confided that when she started to have affairs she was worried that she might become promiscuous. "Didn't that bother you, too?" she asked. I said, "Nope. Never gave it a thought."

For myself and other survivors of my generation, the so-called permissive society is no news. Not if memory serves, and we're truthful about it. There is one difference. It seems to me that sex used to be more fun than it is today, when the copulative act and accessory proceedings often tend to resemble push-button toys with all the romantic aura of a good enema. Also, in addition to the casualness of today's sex, there is too pedantic an attitude toward technique and too little emphasis on emotion. For instance, I pick up a magazine and read an article all about exercises you are supposed to do every day. Here's just one: Lie on your back, take a tampon in its cardboard cylinder, insert it up your rectum, contract your rectum and count to eight slowly. Release. Contract again and repeat count. Release. Contract. Count. Keep it up, with no cheating. Do this five times daily.

Then there is another exercise described in a sex instruction book in which a doctor reveals that women have a pelvic muscle which sounds like a prehistoric monster, the pubococcygeus, and we should exercise it by contracting it ten or more times each hour that we're awake.

These are only two examples from books and magazines streaming off the presses every month, year in and year out, to teach us what to do in bed, and if we followed them all, we sure as hell wouldn't have any time left even to see the men in our lives, much less spend any time in bed with them. In *The Sensuous Woman*, you may remember that the author, "J", wrote: "Set aside several hours a week for masturbating." She added that the minimum number of orgasms at each session should be three or four, "and you should try for ten to twenty-five." Twenty-five? Oh come on now, "J".

Thus, for the modern girl there's never an idle moment all day long. Brush your hair a hundred times, put egg mask on your face, sit with your elbows in lemon halves, do your isometric exercises, read a Good Book, pluck your eyebrows, do your nails, read at least one daily newspaper so you'll be Well Informed, do your housework, shove a tampon up your rectum five times daily, contracting and counting, practice your French or Spanish lessons, go to your job, plan your dinner, do your marketing, exercise your pubococcygeus ten or more times every hour, prepare the vegetables for the casserole, wash your panty hose . . . Let's see . . . I'm sure there was something else. I've left out something. Oh yes. Masturbate. Gosh, I almost forgot. And be sure to count the number of orgasms. Something else to add up and keep track of, along with calories. Well, that's life and sex today. It's just work, work, work.

This is certainly not the way it used to be. For one thing, we didn't practice exercising our pubowhatchamacallits like so many athletes training for sexual Olympics. Nor did we cram for love affairs with the help of sex manuals diagrammed like correspondence course dance lessons. We were guided by our feelings, our instincts, our susceptible flesh, and if we didn't know every trick in the trade right off the bat, we learned gradually and, most of the time, happily. Sometimes a girl picked up pointers from other girl friends; sometimes she learned from her boyfriend or vice versa. Whichever way, we learned, and we practiced together with men whom we loved at the time, not with cucumbers (cucumbers? Yes, they figure among today's popular coital partners) or electric vibrators. One woman, queried recently by a columnist for a sex magazine, "What was the most fun you ever had in bed?" replied, "My best sexual experience was getting into bed with my electric vibrator. I came twelve times."

I think this is a very sad story. Believe me, electricity and steel can never be an adequate substitute for a man and his flesh. Whipping up an orgasm with all the culinary expertise of making a meringue in your Mixmaster is not what real sex is all about. Virtuosity and technique are simply not enough by themselves alone. True sexual ecstasy is inextricably involved with mind and heart. It is not just physiological. (Even whales fall in love and have been known to follow their mates unto death on a beach.) And by the involvement of the mind I don't mean the currently popular myth that bizarre fantasies can enhance your sex life. When a man has been making love to me, I have never pretended that he was a Doberman pinscher.

Romantic sex is more fun than matter-of-fact, technically expert sex. In my day, we made it a big deal, sex with a capital S, aureoled with literary and poetic connotations. The tentative overtures of courtship, the preliminaries to the act itself—we drew them out, prolonged and intensified the anticipation, not wham bam and to bed we go. I don't mean just roses and love notes and candlelit dinners, drinks with names like "Black Velvet" (does anyone today drink champagne and Guinness?), a restaurant violinist playing "La Vie en Rose" to you at your table, summoned by the new man in your life. We had all those, but there was, also, the excitement of small moments too often taken for granted today. The first time your hands touched as he lit your cigarette, or the electrifying touch of his hand on your bare arm. Dancing cheek to cheek, your bodies pressed so close together you could feel his erection, your feet barely moving, slowly, slowly, to the music, your body so faint with desire you could scarcely totter back to the table when the orchestra stopped playing. Our dancing was a far more sexual experience than today's dances, which are not sexual at all, really—just lively calisthenics.

We didn't hurry. I remember my first meeting with a Hungarian artist, Vertès, who came from Paris to work for us when I was an editor on *Vanity Fair* magazine. It was at an office luncheon, and we sat at opposite ends of the table. Our eyes met, and I thought, "I am going to sleep with this man." I knew it. He knew it. But we didn't rush it. Because I could speak French, I had the job of showing him New York and we went out together night after night. We didn't kiss or caress. We waited, savoring the knowledge that eventually we would go to bed. He was a great verbal seducer. He could almost cause a woman to have an orgasm by what he said to her and the way he said it. Furthermore, he was as accomplished in action as in speech.

Although I believe it's healthy to eliminate all hypocrisy or guilt about the human body, I still tend to think that men and women who are accustomed to seeing naked bodies everywhere they turn are perhaps missing the sexual excitement that used to come when you first saw each other nude, or the thrill of having a man undress you. Even the glimpse of a slightly low-cut gown—what used to be called décolletage—could turn a man on. I can remember when Faye Emerson's cleavage, as displayed on early television, was the talk of the country.

We could do a lot with our eyes, too. Both men and women were experts at giving a sexually expressive look. You know the old saying, "He undressed her with a glance"? It was true. I even knew one woman who claimed that with her eyes alone she could bring a man to the verge of climax. She did it by looking directly into his eyes and concentrating, like Uri Geller bending a fork. (In fact, I don't know why I'm being so coy about it. It was me.)

As for the magic vagina, we knew something about that, without the aid of exercise manuals. My first real lover, back in the mid-Twenties, was a newspaper reporter in Syracuse. He was an Irishman born in England, where his father was a bricklayer.

(With remnants of Vassar snobbery, I asked him, "A *bricklayer?* What do you mean?" and he replied, "I mean he laid bricks, one on top of the other, and another one on top of that.") The family had emigrated to Buffalo, New York. At the age of sixteen, my Jim had gone into a Jesuit seminary near Poughkeepsie to study for the priesthood. At twenty, he decided he didn't have the true vocation, so he left, taught Latin and Greek at St. Francis Xavier's in New York and eventually drifted into newspaper work. He knew all about the magic vagina bit, which he certainly didn't learn in the seminary. He was a marvelous man from whom to take guidance in the art of love—tactful, tender, patient, passionate. When I compare his attitude with the belligerent emphasis on sexual technique adopted by many of the present manuals and by much of feminist literature, I can only conclude that they are surely missing a lot today. My own feeling is that the end result of their interminable arguments over the relative merits of clitoral versus vaginal orgasms (indeed, many of them deny that there even is such a thing as the latter, although I am happy to be able to inform them that they are dead wrong) will be to paralyze men into permanent impotence. There is nothing that impairs a man's sexual performance quicker than any suggestion that he's not doing it right ("Not *there,* you idiot!") and it is unfortunate that some of the instructions and pronouncements today are enough to make the average man approach bed as if it had been declared a disaster area. Most men at one time or another experience feelings of sexual insecurity and need to be treated with tact, rather than the blunt truth. A man's inadequacy in bed is immediately apparent physically; a woman's is not. As a university professor I used to know once put it, vulgarly but succinctly, "It is a lot easier to open your legs than it is to get, and maintain, an erection." I would think that it would be to a woman's advantage in the long run to make her bedfellow feel he's wonderful, rather than the opposite, which can only have the effect of deflating him—literally. He may not do things right at first, but making love is not solely an aptitude test. For instance, if he tries to please you by going down on you, it doesn't help matters to tell him he doesn't have to go at it like a beaver building a dam. There are subtler ways of helping him to improve his technique. Love and kindness are more important than a Whizz Kid technique. You don't have to be Heifetz to play the violin and enjoy it. Similarly, you can enjoy sex without a diploma from a sex therapy course. The main thing that makes a girl or a man good in bed is if you're crazy about each other. At least, this used to be true for both sexes and probably still is. If we were mad about a man, all he had to do was lay his hands on us. As for men, there is nothing more seductive than a girl who responds with a show of warmth and appreciation. It is love that turns people on, not just technique. If he's more interested in your sexual technique than in the essential you, it isn't worth it. If technique is what counts most, then the sexual soloists with their vibrators, cucumbers, etc., would of course get a high rating, although it is doubtful if many great poems would be inspired by a woman's affair with herself. Sexual narcissism is better than necrophilia, but both are a rejection of that great natural drive—the passionate coupling of two live human beings, male and female.

Sometimes we were in love, or thought we were. Sometimes we weren't but we pretended to be, because it enhanced and dramatized the sex act. We were romantic, yes. We wanted sex with all the trimmings of compliments and courtship. We wanted to be told that we were loved, even if we didn't believe it. But we were not prissy. We made love in bed, in cars, in fields, on the floor, on chairs, on tables, in the shower, in the cramped quarters of trains and ships, even, on occasion, in the back booths of restaurants. We made love standing, sitting, lying, and, as the old ditty goes, if we'd have had wings we'd have made love flying. All this, when most of us had never heard of the *Kama Sutra*. Indeed, until ten years ago, I thought it was a religious book like the Koran.

However, we regarded sex as an intensely private and intimate affair. We didn't approve of wife swapping or group sex or the type of orgy in which everyone is up for grabs, a sexual version of Tinkers to Evers to Chance—even though these activities existed at the time. There is really not much that is very new in the field, although the more aggressively groovy young people today seem to think they've invented some of their sexual fringe benefits. They haven't. Vibrators, for instance. The irrepressible Viva, that wicked wit who achieved an elegantly randy notoriety in Andy Warhol movies, blew the whistle on several prominent personalities in her book *Super Star*, flimsily disguised as fiction. Among those she portrayed was the daughter of the former head of one of America's publishing empires, a young woman who was once married but who now divides her sex life between girl friends and her ever-loving vibrator—apparently tape-recording each encounter. When I lived in Havana in the Thirties, a Russian countess there was so addicted to her electric vibrator that she pestered her acquaintances by carrying it around with her and plugging it into their outlets, causing Jim Kendrigan of the University of Havana to complain to me, "She's running up my electricity bills!" As far as I'm concerned, this type of sexual solo holds no appeal, as I am so wary of electricity I won't even sleep under an electric blanket and am apprehensive of being electrocuted every time I screw in a light bulb.

Even the wilder, kinkier shores of sex were explored long ago. Take dogs. When I was a newspaper reporter in the Twenties, there was a co-ed at Syracuse University who was rumored to have given birth to a puppy. I'm sure this was untrue, but it was bruited around the newspaper offices in town, and she was expelled from the university, allegedly, so the gossip ran, for having been too affectionate with a collie. During the same era, there was another truly horrible scandal about a couple, both married, who were having a clandestine affair in which they were sometimes joined by the lady's dog, who had been trained as a participant. One night the two lovers and their pet were on the man's cruiser making a night of it, when Rover became overenthusiastic and bit the man's balls off. He bled to death because they were too embarrassed to call for help. When they finally got in touch with a doctor I knew (who told me the story), it was too late. The whole ghastly episode was treated in the papers as an unsolved murder, with no mention of Rover.

Nor are today's live sex shows involving bestiality, as in Copenhagen, a new twist. In Singapore in the Twenties there were exhibitions of donkeys copulating with women; in Havana there was a famous dog nicknamed Old Dog Tray, a performer in brothel shows; and British army officers in the Far East and the Middle East used to have intercourse with chickens, twisting the chickens' necks at the moment of orgasm, which supposedly caused a contraction similar, I guess, to the magic vagina. Recently, I was describing this to a friend with whom I had been discussing my view that there's nothing really new. When I told the part about killing the chicken by twisting its neck, my friend asked, "Why? So the chicken wouldn't tell?"

A few years ago, England broke out in a rash of sex shops that sold a variety of instruction manuals, erotic literature, photographs, and, especially, a fascinating assortment of attachments for both males and females, ranging from elaborate dildos and tinkling bells to suspend from the male organ to other ingenious artifacts of phallusmagoria. The shops were the talk of the town and everybody seemed to think their wares were great new inventions of the permissive society. But back in the Thirties, the Japanese were celebrated for their sex shops that sold the same things, including life-size rubber dolls that could be blown up and used as bedmates and sexual partners. The Japanese also did a brisk business in penis bells, apparently an old but, to me, hilarious sexual device. Raymond Bret-Koch, a French artist I knew when I worked for Condé Nast, told me that Cardinal Richelieu used to wear little silver bells on his penis when he made love.

As I have said, even the magic vaginas aren't new, although we didn't develop them by solitary exercise. Don't worry if you can't do it. Any run-of-the-mill vagina is better than no vagina at all. I think it was in the early Forties that I picked up a magazine in the office of Planned Parenthood, where a friend with whom I was having lunch was publicity director. I was waiting for her and started to glance through this medical magazine when I came to an article called "False Vaginas," a catchy title if ever there was one. I have always remembered the first sentence: "It is very disconcerting to a young woman to discover on her wedding night that she has no vagina."

Naturally, I read on. It seemed that this was not as rare as one might think. The article mentioned that Elizabeth I of England, known as the Virgin Queen, may indeed have been a virgin, not from choice but because she had no other option. Various case histories were described, as well as the fact that false vaginas could be constructed. (When I told this to another magazine editor, she said, "If you find out where, let me know. I could use a new one.")

That was over thirty-five years ago. Last year, I read in *The Times* of London that a European doctor had successfully transplanted a vagina. It seems that his patient had none of her own and she had been married for almost a year. Her husband, understandably, wanted an annulment. Desperate, the wife went to this surgeon. It was the first known operation of its kind, and the donor was the girl's mother. This reminds me of a series of personal medical case histories that ran in an American magazine years ago. The first one was called "I Gave My Kidney to My Brother." I thought that took the cake, but now I can foresee an article entitled "I Gave My Vagina to My Daughter," or perhaps people will carry with them cards donating vaginas, as well as eyes or kidneys, in case of accident. Would-be donors, do not rush. Although this particular transplant was successful and the same doctor has since performed at least one other, most false vaginas are still constructed in the same old-fashioned way. So let Mom keep hers.

There is one thing new in sexual mores and that is today's bisexual chic. Let me rephrase that. What is new about it is that it is openly admitted, that it's the stylish, trendy thing to be. We can read in books, magazines, newspapers, that practically every famous person, past or present, was or is bisexual or homosexual. It has become fashionable to admit it and if you can't truthfully claim to be bisexual yourself, the next best thing is to reveal that one, or both, of your parents was.

It has been going on for eons, although not something previously widely bruited about publicly. History is full of it, even though we are never taught this in school, but then, most of what we are taught about history in school is lies, apart from names and dates. (I still remember that the battle of Teutoburg Forest was in 9 A.D., and a fat lot of good this has done me.) Fourteen out of fifteen of the first Roman emperors were bisexual (the odd man out was Claudius) with, for the most part, a preference for their own sex, although Augustus added a tinge of incest by having an extra affair with his bald granddaughter Julia, who was also sleeping with the poet Ovid, likewise a bisexual, and a jolly time was had by all. . . . Alexander the Great had his adored boyfriend Hephaestion, who was devastated when Alexander married, and Alexander's father, Philip of Macedon, was murdered by one of his ex-lovers. . . . Julius Caesar was notoriously a dab hand with both sexes in bed; Ivan the Terrible kept his painted catamites at court in addition to his mistresses; Edward II and other early English kings had both boyfriends and wives; Richard the Lionhearted was mostly homosexual, although he occasionally varied the routine with his wife or a girl friend; Queen Christina of Sweden was bisexual; and so on down the line.

There is a difference between the homosexual who gets married and manages to father a child and the usually heterosexual husband and father who now and then likes the boys. I'm not about to go into the various nuances of who does what to whom, except to say that the new bisexual chic does not include the gay lads who become the pets of wealthy older women, sometimes legally adopted by them, sometimes married by them. You can see these commercially idyllic couples all over, from Rome and New York to Puerto Vallarta and St.-Tropez. I suppose these women are lonely and they don't have the inner resources to live without escorts, companions, playmates. They keep wanting to go to the party. I always feel that sooner or later, if their young men don't get the sapphire cuff links or the polo ponies or the cars they want, they will make some snide remark about how an old bag ought to be grateful. I couldn't do it because I have too much self-respect and pride—or maybe it's vanity. When younger men make passes at me, and they still do, once in a great while, I am sure they must think I'm a rich old American. I don't even want to have dinner with them, much less go to bed. However, that's only my personal reaction. If other older women can enjoy as well as afford their younger men, why not? Is it possible these women kid themselves into thinking that their young men are with them for any other reason except their money?

As for young women who marry homosexuals, they may be in love or they may have practical reasons. In the case of the homosexual who marries and has children, there is the possibility that he may not be as competently bisexual as he appears. When his wife gives birth, it is assumed that the paternity is his, an assumption not necessarily correct, although in many instances the child actually is the husband's, if sometimes to his own surprise. We all know of famous actors, writers, painters, musicians, politicians and, especially in Britain, more titled scions than you can shake a stick at, who are married and have children but whose sexual preference is for their own gender.

As for the normally heterosexual husband who fancies another man now and then, this is being brought out into the open more, instead of being swept under the rug, as in the past. It's as prevalent in America as anywhere else and among the most respectable exponents of civic virtue as well as among the swingers. I have a homosexual friend of vast experience—he's now in his mid-seventies—and he once told me that he was convinced that 99 per cent of American men have had, or will have, at least one homosexual experience, given the opportunity. I doubt if the figure is that high for women, although it's creeping up fast. The acknowledgment of this is one thing today's young people have done to clear the air, just as they've freed themselves from all the hang-ups earlier generations had about oral sex. They're getting rid of the hypocrisy, the lies, the guilt—if also some of the romance—with which my generation was brought up. It's healthier if sexual variations are admitted and accepted. Sometimes this results in a marriage of convenience and compatibility, in which both spouses continue to carry on with their own sexes: Cole Porter and his wife, Linda, come to mind, or the former fashion model, now an ultra-chic member of le tout Paris set, about whom a mutual friend said to me, "She's a lesbian who married a fag and they're divinely happy because they have no sexual problems at home."

Everyone knew about Noel Coward but what everyone doesn't know is that at least four other famous British actors are bisexual, three of them husbands and fathers. In fact, in England it is easier to pick out those men who are not bisexual (and you can't even be sure—I almost said cocksure—about them). As for women homosexuals, there's nothing new about them, either, except that they're admitting it publicly more often than back in the days when Radclyffe Hall wrote The Well of Loneliness. Coco Chanel was known to be bisexual. Her famous love affairs with the Duke of Westminster and other rich and titled men were varied by amorous episodes with her favorite models and young actresses, and she had a long-lasting liaison with the wife of a celebrated Spanish painter, a passionate affair that only ended with the death of the Spanish woman. Prior to the present day, the best know bisexual women were usually actresses: Tallulah, of course, and, among the rest, the two top Hollywood sex symbols and glamour queens who were found together flagrante delicto by the singer husband of one of them, which put an end to that marriage. There is also a fabulous blond siren who has counted among her lovers some of the most devastating men of the century—actors, writers, directors, publishers, artists—but who has also been noted for her affairs with women. In fact, some friends of mine once saw her get in a physical, hair-pulling brawl with another lesbian over a girl in a Paris nightclub.

Some more complicated relationships occur among those who are considered the most sophisticated. A woman who should know, because she moves in those circles, was relating to me why a world-famous French sex kitten film star left her first husband. "Well, of course, he's bisexual," she began. This has become such an obligatory phrase in any discussion of sex today that I just said "Uh-huh" and waited. "But she is, too, sort of," my friend went on. "How can you be 'sort of'?" I wanted to ask, but I kept quiet. "She left him because she didn't like using a dildo." "Would you mind repeating that?" She repeated it. It took a second or two for it to sink in, because this type of topsy-turvy relationship is difficult for me to figure out, even by diagram. Let's see now. If A equals husband and B equals wife, and B wears an artificial phallus to make anal love to A, then does A become the wife and B the husband, or are they both lesbians? Or what? Hesitantly, I asked my friend a final question: "If that was what he wanted, why didn't he get a man to fuck him?" "Because he loved his wife," my friend said.

My own bisexual experiences are so modest that they scarcely merit the term. I had a boarding-school crush on an older girl who had long black hair, blue-green eyes, a voluptuous figure and, I now realize, looking at her photograph in the school yearbook for 1924, a double chin at the age of seventeen. She was the first female I ever heard swear and I thought she was devilishly sophisticated, as well as ravishing. I wrote passionate and awful poems to her, calling her a goddess and lauding her somewhat matronly beauty; she swore she would love me forever; and we used to kiss each other on the mouth, not even what were then called "soul kisses." We were, I suppose, physically infatuated, but we were also chaste. We didn't know what lesbians were or what they did, and if we had—well, I don't honestly know. . . . (She turned out in later life to be the adult Girl Scout leader in her New England community and a pillar of the church.)

I've had women make passes at me but I've never felt the least urge to respond. Aside from the fact that I've been too busy with men, there is another reason I could never be actively bisexual, even if I were attracted to a woman, which I never am. A woman's genital region is, how shall I phrase it?—less accessible than a man's. I could never put my face there. I have made oral love to men—they are easier to get at—and they have to me, although I always preferred straight old-fashioned fucking. But women are, well, messier, especially Anglo-Saxon women who have not been brought up with a bidet in every bathroom.

My one real bisexual experience was with a woman whom I had known for about six years. We first met when we were reporters on the same Syracuse newspaper. We used to lunch together, occasionally dine in a restaurant, ride horseback on weekends. I never went to her home nor she to mine. She was married to a man much older than herself, but she never discussed her private life. I wouldn't have dreamed of mentioning anything personal to her. In fact, I was careful to mind my p's and q's and not to say anything that might offend her refined sensibilities. She was reserved, intelligent and, above all, ladylike. Her voice was always low, her manner gentle and dignified, her dress conservative—never anything too chic or conspicuous—and her make-up never more than a faint trace of lipstick, a touch of powder. Short, with a rather dumpy figure, she was pleasant-looking rather than pretty. After we had known each other a couple of years, she got a job in New York doing public relations for the Salvation Army and at the time it seemed to me the role for her, right in character. We wrote to each other, casual, impersonal letters, and when I, too, went to New York a year later, we saw each other on the same level as before. We were friends but not intimate friends. I knew vaguely that she was in love with a newspaperman in Albany and hoped to marry him, as indeed she eventually did, but we never discussed men the way you usually do with your women friends. She left the Salvation Army job to become publicity director for one of the oldest and most prestigious publishing firms in America. I was a magazine editor, and we continued our agreea-

ble, but curiously remote, sort of friendship, meeting occasionally
for lunch or dinner, when we discussed books, writers, the theater.
Then, one afternoon after work, we met for cocktails in the
lounge bar of the Barclay. She suggested we have stingers, a lethal
drink made of equal parts of brandy and white crème de menthe.
I'd never had any before and I thought they were delicious. She
kept suggesting that we have another and another and another.
Whenever I said anything about dinner, she would say gently,
"Oh, why don't we have just one more?" I was surprised because,
unlike me, she wasn't much of a drinker. It is probable that I was
having more stingers than she was, but I didn't realize it. We
spent the evening there and the next thing I knew, we had taken
a taxi to her apartment on Gramercy Park, where, to my amazement, she took off all her clothes, gently but firmly suggesting
that I do the same. I wasn't shocked as much as astonished—and
embarrassed, too, because I'd known her so many years. I was also
very drunk. She drew me to the bed and there ensued a frantic
and awkward coupling. I remember that she kept whispering,
"Didn't you know, you fool? Didn't you guess?" (I sure didn't,
lady!) I finally staggered to my feet, got dressed in a blur of dis-
belief and took a taxi home. I never saw her again. Perhaps she
was as embarrassed as I was. She has been dead for many years, or
I wouldn't mention the episode.

After that, I decided, more than ever, to stick to men. With
men, I knew where I was at. That one caper happened over forty
years ago and certainly isn't much to write about today, when everyone else is letting it all hang out. Merle Miller has written
about his homosexual experiences, and so have Emlyn Williams,
the Honorable David Herbert, Robin Maugham (he gets extra
points for writing also about those of his uncle, W. Somerset
Maugham) and Kate Millett. Evelyn Waugh's diaries tell us
about high jinks in the British upper-class ambisexual set of the
Twenties and Thirties, and dozens of other revelations are in
print or in progress. The gasser of them all was Nigel Nicholson's
Portrait of a Marriage, in which he revealed that both his parents
were homosexuals, himself and his brother notwithstanding. Most
of his book deals with his mother's mad affair with Violet
Trefusis (daughter of King Edward VII's mistress, Mrs. Keppel),
as described in his mother's diary, which he discovered in a glad-

stone bag in the attic of the old family castle. (Never keep your diaries in your old family castle. Throw them in the moat.) His mother may have been hot stuff in the sack with Violet, but the excerpts from her diary are schoolgirlish gush (worse than the poems I used to write to my Bradford boarding-school crush), full of exclamation points: "She's mine! She's mine! She's mine!" Both ladies were married but they kept running away together, with their husbands running after them, God knows why. Nicolson's father, Harold, a diplomat and onetime member of Parliament, was busy enough having affairs with his own sex. The mother also had lesser romances with other women, among them the writer Virginia Woolf, who seems to have had an oddly nonsexual marriage. That whole Bloomsbury literary set in London was a hotbed of intramural sex. It's not their morals to which I object. It's their smug conviction of their own superiority. They were appalling snobs.

Bisexual or homosexual, it's nothing new, except that it has become fashionable, although back in the Thirties, Alexander Woollcott's secretary used to answer the telephone by saying, "This is Mr. Woollcott's private pederast." However, we take it more for granted today. As a young girl said to me recently, "Isn't everyone?" Well, no. Not everyone. After all, it's not compulsory. You are free to choose, as I suppose we always were. I chose men.

I like men because they are *male*. I like the way men walk, the way they light cigarettes, the way they stand at bars, the way they talk. I've never particularly been attracted by men who are too handsome or the clean-cut collegiate kind we used to call the Arrow Collar type. Some of my lovers looked terrible when they were undressed, but that wasn't what mattered. Men can have skinny legs, double chins, potbellies, wrinkles, and still be sexually magnetic. I was fond of all the men with whom I slept, either fond of them or else strongly attracted to them physically. I never went to bed with any man for material gain or for any other reason than my own liking and desire. My affair with Condé Nast had nothing whatsoever to do with my job as editor of one of his magazines. I maintained a strict separation between office and bedroom except one time when I was spending a weekend with him at the Atlantic Beach Club on Long Island. We were having breakfast, Condé wearing just his shorts and I in bra and panties.

We started to argue about some editorial policy and unconsciously I slipped into my office role. "But Mr. Nast," I said, and then stopped, realizing the incongruity, under the circumstances, and Condé got up and came around to me, laughing. He put his arm around me and kissed my cheek. "Darling, funny Helen," he said.

The number of my lovers seems rather picayune by modern standards. Looking back, I'm amazed at the number of men with whom I did not go to bed, the ones I liked and went out with, but to whom I said no. Why did I choose some and reject others? I don't really know. As Jean Rhys wrote, "How on earth can you say why you love people? You might as well say you know when the lightning is going to strike." And, long before her day, Conrad wrote in 1907, in *The Secret Agent*, of "an impulse as profound, as inexplicable and as impervious as the impulse which directs a man's preference for one particular woman in a given thousand."

Most of my lovers remained my friends long after our intimacy ended. I remember when one of the first ones, a man I hadn't seen for twenty-five years, telephoned me in May 1957. I had been happily married for eighteen years and was living in Greenwich Village with my husband, Jack, and our two children. The lover's name was Jack, too, and he was a top advertising salesman on *The New Yorker*. When he called, he said, "Tomorrow is an anniversary of ours." I didn't know what he meant, and I said so. He explained. "It is just thirty years ago tomorrow that Lindbergh flew the Atlantic, and that was the day I first met you." He wanted me to have lunch with him. I asked my husband and he said he thought I ought to go, and that it was quite a compliment. I think so, too.

Condé Nast and Bernard M. Baruch remained my friends—and also my husband's—until death. Many others are now dead, too, but I remained on amicable terms with several survivors, including my first husband until his death within the past year. He used to telephone from time to time to see if I was all right, or drop in for a chat. Surprisingly, my Latin American lovers also remained good friends, even inviting me to their homes to meet their wives, an unusual tribute of respect in their countries.

I feel that you never really know a man until you are lovers. It was Robert Browning who wrote: "God be thanked, the meanest of His creatures Boasts two soul-sides, one to face the world with, One to show a woman when he loves her."

I'm glad I'm not young today because I'm not sure I could hack it by modern standards. I think I was fortunate to have lived when I did, and I am grateful for what I had. I remember my lovers with affection, some more so than others. I do not regret a single one.

Chapter Five

———— ✦ ————

WHY I DON'T WANT TO BE A SANDHOG

I have never wanted to be a man. I've never envied men, except for the fact that they can stand at a bar among strangers and start up a conversation about sport, politics, the weather, and soon they're buying each other drinks and it's all perfectly normal and matey, whereas if a woman did the same, they'd think she was trying to pick them up—and most of the time they'd probably be right.

Offhand, I can't think of any other advantage men have over women. Even as a child I neither resented nor emulated boys. I wasn't a tomboy. I didn't want to play baseball or climb trees or set off firecrackers. I not only liked being a girl; I preferred it. Girls didn't have to fight or pretend to be brave. When I was three, living in a small country village, my occasional playmate was the boy next door. We were sent one day with a basket of doughnuts as a gift to a neighbor who owned a dog with a loud bark. I've always been afraid of dogs—I'm a cat lover—and on this errand I persuaded my playmate to walk ahead while I trailed behind at a cautious distance. On our return, my grandmother, who had watched our progress down the road, asked why I didn't walk with Everett. "Well," I replied, "I made him go ahead because I thought if the dog wants to bite anyone he can bite Everett."

Even at that age I could see the advantages of being female.

There is a great welter of literature today to prove that men have always treated women like dirt and that women, by and large, have submitted to their tyranny because, although miserable in their slavery and indignant at their subjugation, they were helpless to do anything about it. That's what the books say. My own theory is that women were not quite so exploited as they now claim to have been. I have a suspicion that down through the ages they have deliberately found certain practical advantages in "inferiority" and that at any given moment, had they chosen to do so, as indeed many of them have done, they could have called the bluff. Throughout the centuries they have proved over and over again that, given the talent or ability, plus the drive (and this is perhaps the key factor), they can do just about any job men can do. That they have not done so in greater numbers has been more often a matter of personal choice rather than denial of opportunity. The majority have opted for the traditional satisfaction and benefits of the female role, and even the more ambitious have usually been content to exercise matriarchal power in subtler fashion than declared overt competition with men. Throughout history, women have manipulated men.

Feminist I am not. Feminine I am. When I was young I didn't want to be Amelia Earhart or Babe Didrickson Zaharias or Sarah Schuyler Butler. I didn't even want to be Garbo. I wanted to be Ruby Keeler, have pretty legs, wear black velvet shorts with a ruffled white blouse, tap dance and shake my curls. Or Alice Faye. I wanted to be cute, adorable, cuddly—the kind of a girl men protect and pamper and call Baby. I never was, but I didn't do too badly with what assets I had, although I was hardly a bona fide *femme fatale*. Did men regard me as a sexual object? I sincerely hope so. Looking around on subway or bus or street, I have often thought, "How very sad to be a really homely girl and know that all your life no passing man is ever going to look at you and think, 'I wish I had a piece of that!'"

A few years ago I was invited to a business lunch in London given by the editors of *Nova*, a magazine now defunct. They were planning an issue on the theme of how women feel when they reach the age of thirty. The idea was that I would write the lead article, a flattering suggestion in view of the fact that I was then over sixty. (As it turned out, I didn't write it.) The lunch was attended by seven women and one man. I was seated between this male editor and Sally, an attractive woman writer in her early thirties who glared at me biliously every time I opened my mouth. The rest of us were chattering and laughing and enjoying ourselves but throughout the three-hour lunch, Sally never smiled once. She was a devout women's libber and I have found that one of their more unattractive characteristics is that they are generally sourpusses.

At some point during the discussion, the editor of the magazine asked me how I had felt when I was thirty. I replied that it was the best year I ever had. "In what way?" "It was the year I met Jack Lawrenson, whom I later married, but it was also the year I was most popular, the year more men fell in love with me than ever have before or since. . . ." Sally, the women's libber, interrupted. "Is *that* what you think makes a good year?" she demanded in a tone so venomous that I was startled. "Well—er—uh," I mumbled. "I think every woman likes to feel that she's attractive to men." "How very feminine of you," Sally sneered, adding, "And I don't mean that as a compliment."

Since then, I have frequently come up against this antagonism, especially during an American publicity tour I made in the summer of 1975 in connection with my autobiography, *Stranger at the Party.* The fact that I had always liked men and had happy relationships with them infuriated feminist women. They seemed to assume that any woman who likes men automatically hates women. "It is obvious that she hates women" was a phrase that cropped up in book reviews, a figment of distorted prejudice. It so happens that my closest friends are all women who have been my friends for anywhere from ten to fifty years, or more, with three of them dating from 1922, 1923, and 1924 respectively. They have always loved and admired men. The women I do dislike are women who hate men.

From that summer I remember three encounters in particular. One was after a radio interview, when the young woman sound engineer began to shout at me belligerently, attacking me for views I had expressed during the interview. She followed me all the way down to the street, yapping spitefully like an angry terrier. The gist of her complaint was that men oppress women, men prevent women from getting any jobs except as secretaries, men are tyrants, men are beasts. Her clincher was that she knew a male employer who said to a girl, or so she claimed, "You sit on the toilet. You can sit to type." I couldn't resist asking her, "What do you want to do—stand up to type and stand up to go to the toilet?" If she was reporting accurately, it was a rude and stupid thing for any man to say, but I'm sure he had provocation.

The second incident was when a fashion model said to me categorically, "Women get all the shitty jobs." Like fashion-model? Most of the more vociferous feminists are white, middle-class, well-educated women who have never known backbreaking manual labor themselves or anyone who has been close to it. When they polemicize about women getting the "shitty" jobs, they have in mind secretarial or clerical work, and they never give a thought to the kind of jobs men get, the millions of men, for example, who work in coal mines or clean sewers or operate pneumatic jack drills. What these women want is to be The Boss. They don't want to work on a factory assembly line. They want to be president of the company, ignoring the fact that not all men get the top jobs, either, or even get a chance at them. They're always arguing that some women may be stupid enough to want to do housework but that all women should at least be able to have a choice, as if it ought to be simply a question for the average woman of deciding, "Should I stay home and wash dishes or should I be a Supreme Court Justice?"

There are a few freakish women who, in their mad desire to equal or outdo men at anything and everything, aspire to some of the more unpleasant and physically demanding jobs traditionally done by men. This was brought out during the third episode that I remember from that publicity trip. The editors of New York magazine gave a scrumptious lunch for me in their office, with nine or ten of us at table, of whom four were women members of the editorial staff. Everyone was friendly and so complimentary that I was having a fine time until eventually, toward the end, the inevitable questions surfaced, all asked by the women. Why was I not a feminist? "Because I think it's a phony nonissue." Didn't I believe that women get a lousy deal from men? "No more than men get from women." How could I have stayed home evenings with the children when my husband was out in the bars? "Someone had to stay with them because we couldn't afford a baby-sitter

very often." "But you must have been angry. You must have
hated him," one of the young women insisted. "Certainly not!
When we did go out together we had a wonderful time, but I
couldn't do it every night. For one thing, have you ever tried to
feed Pablum to a baby in the morning when you have a hangover
from staying out drinking till four? I thought not. Besides, what
would I have done, running around the bars by myself? I would
have felt like an idiot. I can't see myself standing at a bar,
watching baseball on the TV, while my husband stayed home. It's
not my style."

The point I want to make, however, is that one woman brought
the discussion to a climax when she told me, as a horrible example
of male injustice, that there was a New York woman who wanted
to build subways. In other words, she wanted to be a sandhog,
working dangerously to dig underground tunnels and going
through a decompression chamber before surfacing, in order not
to die of the bends. She was refused the job, so she went to court
and sued. She lost the case. "There!" said the woman editor tri-
umphantly, "Now what do you think of *that?*" "I think she's a
nut," I said. "She just wanted to get her picture in the papers as
the first woman sandhog."

What normal woman in her right mind would want this kind
of a job? Why on earth should women clamor to be treated like
men? Do they really want their husbands home in aprons while
they rush off to a factory or to a road construction gang? Do they
want to be drafted and sent to war to kill people? Have they any
idea of what this spurious equality they blather about would actually mean in terms of everyday community life? Fortunately, the
majority of women don't agree with them, yet so true is the
maxim "The squeaky wheel gets the grease" that men, cowed by
the stridency of the feminist demands and, in the case of politicians, cagily courting female votes, are outdoing each other in
protestations of support even for such members of the lunatic
fringe as women who apply for jobs as garbage collectors. In 1971
the governor of Colorado signed a bill removing the ban on
women in coal mines, an act greeted with joy by feminist leaders
who have never even seen a coal mine and who would shoot
themselves before they'd work in one. (Can you picture Gloria
Steinem or Betty Friedan digging away at the pit face, miles un-

derground, in passages so narrow they can't stand upright?)
Women were working down in the mines with men long before
the first suffragette, and it's only a few generations ago we
brought them out, in the name of humanity and civilization and
progress. Now, thanks to the feminists, the clock could be set
back. Children used to work in the mines, too, just as children of
five and younger used to work in the mills. Should we go back to
that, as well?

Let me make clear that I support the saner aspects of the movement: the valid claims for legal rights, property rights, equal pay
for equal work, free child-care centers, free abortions and the like.
These can be fought for and won without waging a sex war. Yes,
men are often childish, vain, selfish, cruel, thoughtless and so
forth, but so are women. What makes these liberation activists
think women are easy to live with? They ignore their own faults
and the fact that men and women are human beings who comple-
ment each other, who need each other, and that the adjustment
process of living together is what life's all about.

Although many women's libbers attack me, there are more who
praise me for having been what they call "liberated" over fifty
years ago, way ahead of time. They, too, are wrong. I was no more
liberated than other women and I didn't have to fight for what I
did. A few years ago, before I appeared on a TV interview show in
Boston, an assistant on the show telephoned me to get background material. I gulped when she asked me, "Were you the first
woman journalist?" "Have you never heard of Annie Oakley?"
No, she hadn't.

Far from being the first woman journalist, I was one in a long
series, too many to mention, except briefly. In 1869 Middy Morgan was the first woman reporter on the New York *Times*. For
twenty-three years she covered horse shows, dog shows, racing and
livestock events. In the 1880s Mrs. Florence Finch Kelly was a reporter in Boston and in 1894, Ida Tarbell, who became a famous
journalist, earned the then munificent sum of forty dollars a
week! Agnes Meyer, mother of Mrs. Katherine Graham, the
owner of the Washington *Post* and *Newsweek*, was a newspaper
reporter on the old New York *Sun* back in 1907, before I was
born. A few of the more prominent women journalists in the
Twenties and early Thirties were Irene Kuhn in New York;

Dorothy Thompson, an outstanding foreign correspondent before she became a political pundit; Mildred Gilman, who interviewed, among others, Hermann Göring at the beginning of the Nazi regime. ("In America we're worried about the Jewish question," she told him, to which he replied, perhaps deliberately misunderstanding, "We're worried about it here, too.") During the later Thirties there were, notably, Martha Gellhorn, a correspondent covering the Spanish Civil War, and, in the Fifties, war correspondent Marguerite Higgins. These were all women whose prestige was equal or superior to that of men.

I started work in 1926 as a newspaper reporter in Syracuse, New York, at twelve dollars a week. True, I was probably hired because Bud O'Hara, who owned the paper, used to work for my father, but it wasn't because of this that two years later a rival paper enticed me away with an offer of forty dollars a week, and that I was later offered jobs by Emile Gauvreau and Walter Howie, two famous editors of New York papers. There were other women journalists in Syracuse before I started: Ramona Herdman, Finette Edwards, Gladys Plank. My first few days I wrote church notices and similar stuff, but not for long. I was assigned to stories on equal basis with men. I was never a "sob sister" or a woman's page writer. I covered sewer construction scandals, political conventions, prison riots, fires, murders. Throughout my early professional career I never came up against any resentment from men, nor did men ever try to obstruct me in my work. It was women who did that. I have learned that in any competitive field women can be more vicious, envious and conniving than men. Their stepping stones to success are frequently the heads of other women. They are adept at a deviously unethical infighting that can cause men to blanch in horror.

There are also women today, just as there were in my time, who get ahead by using men sexually, thereby gaining what back in the Thirties Clare Boothe Luce used to call "jungle jobs, the kind you hang onto with your tail." It is seldom, if ever, that men rise to the top by this tactic. As for myself, I did not get my jobs or assignments by making goo-goo eyes at the boss. I got them by being good at my work, not good in bed. When I was twenty-six I was made managing editor of *Vanity Fair* magazine, although the rest of the staff, with one exception, were men. I didn't seek the position or try in any way to get it. It wasn't given to me because I had special pull but because Frank Crowninshield, the editor, thought I was the best available. The only person who resented my promotion and tried to hinder it was the other woman, who I had thought was my friend.

Perhaps the reason male fellow workers on newspapers and magazines forty and fifty years ago were not hostile was because I never tried to diddle them out of their jobs. I didn't compete with men. I worked *with* them. When I went drinking with them I paid my own way, and they accepted me as an equal. Back in the Twenties a Syracuse friend with the splendid name of Bartholomew O'Neill Murphy once took me to an illegal crap game run in an upstairs back room of a rather seedy hotel. When the guard at the door saw me he said, "No ladies allowed." "She's no lady. She's a newspaper reporter," Bart said, and we were admitted.

So don't hand me that malarkey about men keeping women out of jobs because of sex discrimination. By and large, it isn't true today and it wasn't true in my time, or even before. Hundreds of thousands of girls who started as secretaries or in humbler jobs were able to make it to top level. I knew a fifteen-dollar-a-week receptionist who became managing editor, first of *Glamour*, then of *Cue*, and a filing clerk who ended up advertising manager of the Neiman-Marcus store in Texas. In 1895 Edna Woolman Chase began her career by addressing envelopes in the office of the original *Vogue*. She rose from the ranks through merit alone to become editor in chief, turning it into the most famous fashion magazine in the world. . . . Around 1920, Clare Boothe Luce was working in a factory, making paper flowers. In later years she became a secretarial assistant, then magazine editor, successful playwright, congresswoman, American ambassador to Italy. . . . Jacqueline Cochran, raised in near poverty in a southern sawmill town, became a celebrated aviatrix, as they used to be called. She was not the first—Amelia Earhart and Ruth Elder were before her—but in 1953 she was the first woman flyer to break the sound barrier, in an F-86 Sabre jet. She was also a cosmetics tycoon and president of an important New York store. Interviewed in 1975, when she was sixty, she had this to say about the women's liberation movement: "I have never been discriminated against in my life. I think the women complaining they've been discriminated against are the ones who can't do anything anyway."

Women have done almost everything you can name. They have been riveters, archaeologists, trolley car drivers, judges, bank robbers, explorers, stockbrokers, butchers, bullfighters, financiers (look at Hetty Green: no man ever stood in *her* way!), plumbers, jockeys, wrestlers, embalmers and undertakers, legislators, rat catchers, publishers, ambassadors, cabinet ministers, doctors, lawyers, tax experts, scientists, bartenders, auditors and even, some thirty-odd years ago, 6 per cent of the country's professional paperhangers. We have had no woman President yet, but as rulers in other countries they have been just as ruthless and tricky as men, not only in ancient times but in today's world as well. One has only to look at India's ex-Prime Minister, Mme. Gandhi, an oppressive dictator who had 676 political opponents arrested in a single day, many taken straight from their beds to prison, there to be held indefinitely without trial, and who brutally continued to suppress all criticism during her autocratic regime. She got her comeuppance when she finally felt secure enough to permit an election and was soundly defeated by eighty-one-year-old Morarji Desai. Again, take Mme. Bandaranaike, former Prime Minister of Sri Lanka, similarly prone to dispose of anyone daring to question her decisions. Also, it should be noted by ardent feminists that women in positions of power are notably loath to countenance the advancement of any other women in their bailiwicks. The ferociously ambitious Mrs. Margaret Thatcher, as Leader of the Tory Party in opposition to the British government, saw to it that there were few women in her shadow cabinet!

It is true that millions of women are working because they want to do so and they enjoy their jobs, just as millions are working when they had rather stay home. A vast number of working mothers are in professions like teaching, nursing, the social services. This, too, is valid and admirable. My point is that the majority of women do not yearn to be butchers, rat catchers, embalmers, plumbers or the like. Their main interests lie in other directions, namely, home, husband and children. This is anathema to the feminists, whose basic premise is that housework is degrading and that most women abominate it. They are dead wrong. Most women enjoy taking care of their own homes. They may gripe now and then about dishes, dusting and diapers, but few of them would prefer to exchange them for eight hours a day in a factory. They do not feel that be it ever so humble there's no place like an assembly line. Some years ago a Department of Labor survey of working women showed that a typical explanation of their motivation was "Because my husband doesn't earn enough to support our family with the cost of living what it is." They did not say, "Because I want to do a man's job instead of housework" or "Because I'm just crazy about the assembly line."

A woman's home is her own domain. She takes pleasure and pride in running it, fixing it up, planning new curtains, using her best dishes for company, cooking special treats for her family. I have done it all; and I know. There is a sensory delight in putting clean sheets on a bed, in the smell of clothes that have been dried on a line outdoors, in the sight of a pie that comes from the oven looking perfect. I cannot put my hand on my heart and swear that I ever loved washing clothes by hand with a washboard (even the small one trademarked Little Darling) but I have done it and it didn't kill me. There was a period when I did all our family wash, including sheets, our clothing and the children's, even my husband's shirts. I didn't find it detestable drudgery and it certainly never entered my head to feel degraded. I've always liked to iron, ever since I was a child and used to ask to be allowed to do the flat things like handkerchiefs and napkins. In fact—and I trust I won't be stoned in the streets by irate libbers for this confession—I don't hate washing dishes. There is a sense of achievement from dishes all clean and put away, pans shining, the sink scoured. And it sure as hell beats working in factory or office.

I can't sew, but I've often wished that I didn't have to earn a living and had the time to learn how. I'm sure women who can do it must derive a lot of satisfaction from being able to make things, just as I would never sneer patronizingly at women who take part in contests like the Pillsbury bake-off and who are justifiably proud of their ability. Even that early paladin of feminism Simone de Beauvoir has said that "there is a poetry in making preserves . . . cooking is revelation and creation; and a woman can find special satisfaction in a successful cake."

It is laughable for any American women, the most liberated in the world, with all their labor-saving gadgets, electric washing machines, vacuum cleaners, frozen foods, ready-mixes, nonstick pans, and so on, to harangue each other—and men—about what they call the humiliating drudgery of housework. I feel like saying to them, "You fools. You're lucky to have your homes. Millions of women in the world have none, because of floods, earthquakes, tidal waves, cyclones, volcanic eruptions, chemical poisoning of their towns and villages, the devastation of wars still being waged, the ravages of vile regimes that have made home for many women a refugee camp or a prison cell." In their appalling selfishness and their obsession with inflated ideas of their own importance, the so-called liberationists choose to ignore all this and instead to make a fuss over who does the dishes.

Another thing that irritates me about them is their curious attitude toward children. In all their utterances on the subject they seem to regard children only as a hardship, and they are always nattering on about the odious burden of taking care of a baby. Most normal women want children, as is evidenced by the thousands who apply to adopt them because they have none of their own. I believe that there is no substitute for the miracle of giving birth to your own child. However, women who for one reason or another cannot bear children derive enormous happiness from adopted babies; and they adopt them because they *want* to take care of them, they want them in their homes. I read the other day that earwigs are devoted mothers, risking anything to protect their young. I am not willing to concede that female human beings are less maternally dedicated, generally speaking, than earwigs. Yet in a radio broadcast in September 1976, I heard an earnest young woman feminist argue that "any inborn urge for women to reproduce must be phased out." She didn't specify how this would be accomplished.

The feminists seem to forget, or not to know, about love and what happens to a woman when she falls in love. As I have frequently said, "Even the most emancipated career woman can fall in love. . . . Love is caring more for someone else than you do for yourself. When a woman falls madly in love with a man, she wants to wait on him and please him and be bossed by him and make a home for him and bear his child. Anyone who says otherwise is talking rubbish."

Yes, women suffer from what the Latin poet Lucretius over two thousand years ago called "the eternal wound of love." So do men. As an anonymous medieval lady at Eleanor of Aquitaine's court remarked, "Mortal love is but the licking of honey from thorns." This having been admitted, it must also be noted that it is easier to complain about love than to stop it from happening—and who would want to? Only someone like Ti-Grace Atkinson, one of the lodestars of the feminist movement, who was once quoted as saying, "Love has to be destroyed. It's an illusion that people care for each other." If she truly believes this, for whatever personal reasons, that's her problem. Her bitter crusade is a doomed one. Women have always fallen in love and they always will. When they do, everything else becomes unimportant compared with the sight of one man who stands out from all others in a room as if illumined by some magic nimbus, the sound of his voice, the touch of his hand. A woman in love will maneuver conversations with other people in such a way that the man's name will be mentioned, and it rings like a bell in her heart.

There are practically no limits to what she will put up with, no lengths to which she will not go. For example, I think of Carole Lombard giving up the parties and night life she loved and determinedly learning to hunt and shoot and fish, activities she hated. Getting up at four o'clock in the morning in order to sit motionless for hours in a cold, wet wild duck blind was not her idea of a good time, but she did it, over and over again, to please Clark Gable. Jeanne Moreau once told me, "When I am in love, I am a slave. I want a man to dominate me and I will do anything to please him and make him happy." It is Fannie Brice all over again, singing "My Man" and thinking of Nicky Arnstein (*What's the difference if I say I'll go away/When I know I'll come back on my knees some day?*). Or Katharine Hepburn, otherwise the epitome of proud independence, enduring year after year Spencer Tracy's recurring bouts with the bottle. Liza Minelli told me she will never forget the sight of Hepburn sitting on the floor outside Tracy's locked hotel room, pleading with him to let her in, when he was holed up for one of his prolonged periods of solitary drinking.

We've all of us been through it in one form or another. I loathe exercise, but I have walked ninety-two blocks in the early dawn, day after day, with a prizefighter over whom I was briefly swoon-

ing. I suppose I was lucky we didn't have to skip rope all the way.
I never slept with him, either. At the time, I thought it was because he was too puritanical but, looking back, I think he may
have preferred his own sex. . . . And when I was mooning over
Irwin Shaw, I sat with him on the floor throughout an entire Carnegie Hall concert, although I am tone deaf; and many a time I
lay in bed with him, listening to classical music on his phonograph. So eager was I to match his mood that I went to Gus
Schirmer's store in New York and all but asked, "What have you
got good by Beethoven?" I bought several records and my mother
and stepfather, with whom I was staying in Flatbush, were thereafter stupefied to hear me diligently playing Beethoven and
Brahms instead of my usual rumba records. Ah, love. It's funny
and it's marvelous and it's no bed of roses, but I'm sorry for any
woman who has never felt it.

In 1969 I wrote an article about women's liberation. It was
called "The Feminine Mistake," was published in the January
1970 issue of *Esquire* and has been reprinted in several antholo-
gies. At the time, I thought the movement was a stupid fad that
would soon peter out. Instead, it began to snowball, with im-
becilic slogans like "Women are the niggers of today." It
shouldn't take more than a second to realize the ludicrous inaccu-
racy, the shocking obscenity, of any comparison between the position of modern American women and what the blacks have been
through. That particular slogan didn't last long, but there have
been a host of minor asininities enthusiastically adopted, such as
referring to the chairman of a meeting as "chairperson," the evan-
gelical flourish with which "sisters" and "sisterhood" are incessantly spouted, or the increasing use of "Ms." Whenever I see this
last one in print or on a letter, my hackles rise, or would if I had
any. I understand it is pronounced Miz, as in "Miz Helen Lou,
honey, is you-all goin' to de hoe-down?"

Although the silliness is more rampant in America, other countries are catching up. After the Sex Discrimination Act was passed
in England, the Office of Fair Trading issued a bulletin dealing
with conditions under which temporary employees may be hired,
such as, to replace "people having babies." British Rail set about
complying with the act by abolishing women's waiting rooms in
stations and depots, but they had to back down when women

themselves objected. A firm of chartered public accountants wanted to run a full-page advertisement in their trade magazine, depicting a group of bees, the idea being that they were busy as bees. The Equal Opportunities Commission insisted that the advertisement be amended "to give reasonable parity between male and female figures [meaning the bees, as there were no other figures] both in prominence and in numbers," ignoring the fact that to most people all bees look alike. Anyway, as the columnist Bernard Levin pointed out, it is only female bees that do the work of collecting the honey. Miss Betty Lockwood, chairman of the commission, asked a London *Times* reporter, "Why should it always be the woman who takes little Johnny to the dentist?" (I could tell her why. It's because the man of the family is at work, earning the money to pay the dentist.) Around the same time, the vice-chairman of the same commission issued a clarion call demanding that advertisers stop showing women holding up detergents and that educational authorities abolish primary school books showing Mummy in the kitchen and Daddy in the garden.

As in America, these English liberationists are a white, middle-class, elitist group who think of themselves as intellectuals. Most of them are professional women, with the majority writers, editors, or connected in some way with what is called the media. The average workingwoman views them with a mixture of amusement and contempt. When a group of feminists threw their wedding rings in garbage pails, stating that such a ring is "the greatest symbol of the oppression of a woman," one female onlooker was heard to say emphatically, "They must be daft!" while another remarked, "I don't want men's jobs. I'd rather have their seats on buses." I was in London in 1975 when a Japanese housewife, Mrs. Junko Tabei, became the first woman to climb Mount Everest. I took a random poll of women in supermarkets, on the underground, in bus queues. Not one seemed impressed, and when I asked if they would want to emulate her, the typical answer was "You must be joking!"

I cannot understand women who say they'd go crazy if they had to stay at home. I don't want to be a sandhog or an ambassador or a bank president. I am proud to have been a housewife and a mother. I think the feminists are selling themselves short as women. A Parisian woman, formerly the editor of *L'Express*, had this to say a year or so ago: "We don't have twin beds as they do in the United States. Perhaps our husbands don't do dishes but they will buy you a dishwashing machine. . . . We will not have a woman's revolution in France as long as the double bed remains."

So let the feminists cavil all they want. While they're out climbing Mount Everest, I'll be home happily baking a cherry pie.

Chapter Six

HOW NOT TO RISE TO THE TOP

From the beginning, I didn't really want a job. The only reason I went to work was that I had to earn my own living. By the end of my second year at Vassar I decided that I ought not to live off my grandmother any more, the way my parents did, and that anyway she didn't have a lot left. I wasn't going to inherit anything and at that time I had no intention of getting married. Ergo, I must find some way to support myself.

Neophyte writers today often ask me how I became a journalist. I never know what to say. I didn't take any courses; it was not a girlhood ambition; and I hate writing. It is hard, tedious work. Dorothy Parker once told me that she and some friends were talking about what is the most fun in the world, and Robert Benchley said, "The most fun in the world is *not writing*." Many of the professionals I know will go to ridiculous lengths to postpone it. One well-known writer had a deadline to meet and, like most of us, he cannot work with anyone else around, so he sent his wife out to a neighborhood movie, where she sat through a double feature, one of them twice. When she finally went home, she found that her husband had not finished his article but he had polished all the silver, brass, and copper in the house. I myself will suddenly decide to clean the stove or straighten my bureau drawers, to avoid the dreaded moment of sitting down at the typewriter.

True, when I was a child I used to scribble verses, most of

which were hilariously lurid. I sent them off to children's magazines like *St. Nicholas* and *Little Folks,* whose editors sent them
back as fast as they could get the stamps on the envelopes. I was
certainly no Nathalia Crane. One jingle called "The Rape" began,
"He gazed at her body, slim and white,/And within him rose
desire./He stealthily crept near her bed/And his veins burned living fire." Another gem, "The Tenement" (I was twelve and had
never seen a tenement) started off, "Squalor, garbage and dirt.
God! how it smells!" and went on for eight similarly cheery verses.
My absolute favorite was "The Opium Eater." Yes, eater. I had
been dipping into Thomas De Quincey, obviously out of my
depth. The first three stanzas set the scene:

> He staggered into the opium den
> Diseased and wracked with pain;
> His eyes were bleared and bloodshot
> With longing for cocaine.

> On bunks and chairs and floor
> He saw the sleepers sprawling,
> Their faces lustful and greedy,
> Their bodies stinking and crawling.

> Dope-crazed, he clawed at the host.
> "Quick! The opium pipe! God, boy!"
> He got it and then he looked around
> For a woman to enjoy.

Never mind why he went to an opium den if he wanted cocaine. It rhymed, didn't it? Cannily deeming it not quite a suitable topic for *Little Folks,* I sent it to *Harper's.* I imagine it bright-
ened their whole day in the office before they could bring
themselves to part with it and return it to me. After that, I gave
up and confined myself to prose in the form of school themes and
occasional contributions to school magazines, but I had no
dreams of a writing career.

I suppose those first childish efforts were inspired by my om-
nivorous reading, which was nothing if not promiscuous. In addition to devouring every book I could find, I also pored over piles
of old magazines in the attic of my grandmother's house, including *The Theosophical Path,* in which I read with utter incom-
prehension the orphic theories of those early female gurus, Mme.

Helena Blavatsky and Annie Besant, and a periodical (the name of which I have forgotten but I remember it had such tiny print it's a wonder I didn't go blind) that published alluring serials about highborn ladies with alabaster brows and names like Lady Claribel Vere de Vere, who were forever fending off amorous villains. We also had a stack of paperbacks, then rather a pejorative term, by Mary J. Holmes and Ruby M. Ayres. My grandmother rightly described them as trash but nevertheless I read them all, often by flashlight in bed. Ruby M. Ayres, I recently learned, to my surprise, wrote 150 novels and made $60,000 a year, a hefty enough sum for her time to make her commercially equal, relatively speaking, to such modern writers as Jacqueline Susann and Harold Robbins. Even today, sixty years or more later, her books still sell some 17,000 to 20,000 copies a year, updated—cars instead of horse and buggy, mini or maxi skirts instead of bustles— by a British writer named Alan Wyckes, who shares the royalties with the Battersea Dogs Home in London, in accordance with the terms of Mrs. Ayres's will.

It was not writing that occurred to me at Vassar as a way of earning money, but the stage. This was because I always had an exceptional memory and easily learned by heart (what a curious phrase—not learned by mind but by heart) the longest poems as well as prose passages. As a child I had appeared in school plays and Little Theater amateur productions in Syracuse, although I had no burning desire to be an actress. It just seemed the only thing I thought I might be able to do. My Aunt Grace was a friend of the famous musical comedy star Marilyn Miller, then appearing on Broadway in *Sunny*, and she took me backstage to meet her. Marilyn gave me a letter to Rosalie Stewart, the only woman producer on Broadway, who told me, "I can give you a walk-on part right now. But you're so fortunate to be a Vassar student that I think you're crazy not to take advantage of it. Why don't you stick it out there for another year and then come and see me?"

I never went back to her. 'Bye, 'bye, Bernhardt. Obviously, I was not consumed by theatrical ambition. Instead, I briefly considered a few other options. My mother knew a man named Straus who was then head of Macy's and he said he would get me into their training course; I filled out a questionnaire for a job in the New York Public Library on Fifth Avenue at Forty-second Street and received a reply saying there would be an opening in the autumn; I was offered a position as superintendent of a Montessori School in Woodstock, New York. I never followed up any of these, but I went to Europe that summer with my mind made up not to waste any more time at college.

When I returned home to Syracuse in the fall of 1926 I was nineteen and still with no idea of what to do. It was my father who finally suggested I try newspaper work. Why not? He made an appointment for me to see an old acquaintance who owned a paper, and I was hired at twelve dollars a week. It was as simple as that. Not much on which to base helpful advice for any would-be journalists. Rule One: First, find a newspaper publisher who used to work for your father.

I loved my four years on Syracuse newspapers, just as I thoroughly enjoyed my later four years on *Vanity Fair* magazine, but I had nothing of the Get-Rich-Quick-Wallingford spirit. I felt no urge to rise to the top. I have never lusted for power or fame or money. Money is nice and it's also necessary, but having lived through the Wall Street crash of 1929, when multimillionaires lost everything overnight and shot themselves or jumped out of windows, I view the single-minded acquisition of money with considerable skepticism. People with a lot of money always want more and more of it, and then they worry for fear they might lose some of it. I sometimes think of an evening in the Thirties when I was having dinner with Bernard Baruch and his wife in their Fifth Avenue mansion and, apropos of nothing, Bernie remarked, "Poor old Charlie Schwab. He hasn't got a nickel." I thought it was a hyperbole, because when millionaires talk about being broke it usually means they think they can't afford a new yacht. Schwab was, or had been, head of U. S. Steel or some similarly exalted position, so I could scarcely picture him having to take back empty bottles to the delicatessen in order to get carfare to go to his job, a practice not uncommon in my own set. I'm sure he was never reduced to that, but when he died at some later date, I was astonished to read in the papers that Baruch had been right. Although Schwab had once been worth multiple millions, he died insolvent, albeit in Leroy, an expensive private hospital in New York's East Sixties. Anyway, Bernie's comment was a source of cheer to me during lean years when, eating in some cheap restaurant, I would order the prune whip because it was five cents cheaper than the icecream. "Poor old Charlie Schwab," I would think. "He hasn't got a nickel." It bolstered my decision never to become a multimillionaire. Too risky.

When I quit my Syracuse newspaper job and went to live in New York it was the winter of 1930–31. Having previously muffed several opportunities to work on New York papers, there were by then no such positions available. The Depression was under way, with men selling apples on street corners and long lines of the hungry unemployed standing in the cold, waiting for free soup dished out by various charitable groups. I lived in an apartment on East Thirtieth Street, off Fifth Avenue, between two Armenian restaurants. It was a five-flight walk-up and consisted of two rooms, kitchen and small bathroom. I shared it with a girl who worked in a travel agency and two friends from my boarding-school days, one of whom was studying to be a doctor and used to bring home slices of human arms from dissected corpses, looking disconcertingly like liverwurst. The other, having graduated from Wellesley and spent two years as a law student at Columbia, could get no better job than selling men's neckties in Stern's department store. Work of any kind was scarce and pay was minimal. Still, we survived with admirable bounce and cheerfulness. It never occurred to us to feel sorry for ourselves.

I read the New York *Times* want ads and went traipsing around to a slew of agencies. I had no qualifications, no training. By the time I got through admitting that I didn't know shorthand, could only type with two fingers, had no experience as a switchboard operator, and not only couldn't operate something called a Moon Hopkins machine but didn't know what it was, I felt like a bumbling dunce. I could have had a job making toast in a quick lunch but I turned it down because I always managed to burn the toast at home and I didn't fancy doing it in public. I auditioned for some kind of radio work but then never went back for the second appointment. At the final agency I visited, I was just being sent away when the lady called me back and asked, "Have you ever sold books?" I told her yes and gave a flock of fake references, ranging from the Vassar Bookshop to Syracuse stores. She sent me to the Womrath headquarters. Womrath owned a chain of lending libraries, with seventy stores in New York. I filled out a long application, swore to report any employee I found doing anything detrimental to the company, gave my list of phony references and got the job, at $18.50 a week. I had to pay the agency a week's pay, so it wasn't until the end of my fourth week that I received full pay.

In a letter to an ex-Vassar friend I wrote: "I work in shifts, from 9 a.m. to 6 p.m. one week and from 1 p.m. to 9:30 p.m. the next. So far, I have been in nine stores in one month. I get sent from one to the other to fill in. My peregrinations range from 8th Street, the nicest shop because the manager, who is a man, calls me 'Kiddo' and lets me sit down and even read, to Broadway at 112th Street. In my 'home store,' 68th and Madison, the lending library customers include Princess Miguel de Braganza, Mrs. Livingstone French, Mrs. Condé Nast and the like. They come sweeping in with swanky dogs hitched to them, or else send their chauffeurs. The usual routine is to come into the store, which is lined with shelves of books on all sides, and ask, 'What's a good book?' Follow up questions are: 'Is it sad?' 'What's the story about?' We are supposed to knock ourselves out to rent books that are not popular. We had one, *Mère Marie*, that we couldn't persuade anyone to take. My big triumph came one day when I shamelessly unloaded it on a gullible old lady. After she left, the woman store manager cried excitedly, 'Girls! Girls! Miss Brown has rented *Mère Marie!*' The others congratulated me as if I had just won the world high-jump trophy."

Every book in the stores was checked at the end of the day and reports made out on triplicate forms, a process I enjoyed because it dispelled my belief that I could never learn to be efficient. At first, the cash register bothered me because until I learned to step aside, the drawer sprang out and hit me in the stomach. Womraths were too cheap to hire janitors so I had to get there before opening time in order to dust the books, sweep out the store with one of those rectangular brush-brooms street cleaners use, empty the cigarette butts and other trash into wrapping paper and stagger up a flight of stairs to dump it in a back room. On my way to work in the morning I used to see the janitors or porters of other kinds of stores sweeping out with the same type of push broom. I longed to stop and ask them how they managed the corners. I didn't really mind it, though. If they could do it, I could do it, too.

After three months I was promoted to assistant manager at twenty dollars a week. This was half my salary on the Syracuse newspaper but I managed somehow, although peanut butter sandwiches and canned beans figured largely in my diet. Fortunately, I liked them. (I still do.) I was also occasionally taken to dinner by a man named Tom Stix, president of the Book League of America, a book club. He was a tubby, pleasant little man who took me to fashionable speakeasies and to the theater, gave me books, and never attempted any further intimacy than a peck on my cheek when he brought me home. My first date with him was a memorable one. It was the first time I had ever been to a theatrical opening night, the first time I had been out with a man who wore a high silk hat, the first time anyone sent me orchids and the first time I had champagne. However, it was something else that made it a unique experience and one I dare say few others have known.

We had two bottles of champagne with dinner and dallied so long that I didn't have time to go to the ladies' room before the theater. At some point during the first act I had to go to the bathroom. We were sitting in the middle of the third row center. As I looked at all the people on either side of us I didn't have the nerve to try to get out, although if I had known what was coming, I would have walked on their laps to reach the aisle. I suddenly realized, to my horror, that I had started to pee, sitting there in my seat, looking at the stage. I thought I would never stop. Fortunately, my evening skirt was long and full, made of velvet that was absorbent. In those days we wore underclothes, so I had on ruffled crêpe de chine panties and a long silk evening petticoat. Nothing went on the floor but the back of my skirt was sopping wet and felt as if weighted with lead. I didn't know how to break the news, so at intermission I said I'd rather not go out to smoke. I sat there, soggy and flabbergasted, trying to act nonchalant and wishing I were dead.

When the play ended, I still couldn't bring myself to tell Stix, so I draped my evening cloak over my rear and meekly went with him to a nightclub where he had a reservation. He kept asking me to dance and I kept refusing. Finally, I said, "I can't dance." "Ho-

ho-ho," he laughed genially. "I can't believe that. Come on now, let's try this fox trot," and he grabbed my arm. So then I told him. He looked dumbstruck but then he began to laugh. He said it was the funniest thing he had heard and he couldn't get over what he called my Olympian stoicism. I'm sure it was one of his favorite anecdotes for years to come.

I worked at Womraths six months and was then informed by the superintendent that they would make me manager of my own store, at twenty-five dollars a week. I promptly quit and went off to spend the summer with my grandmother at her place in the Thousand Islands. My next job was as much of a surprise to me as it was a contrast to my last one. Through a friend of a friend I heard about a vacancy on *Vanity Fair* magazine. I was hired after sending in some sample captions, followed by three interviews. Although it only paid twenty-five dollars a week at first, it was a lot more entertaining than Womraths. By the time the magazine merged with *Vogue* four years later, I was managing editor. There was no suitable place for me on *Vogue*, so Condé Nast suggested that I try Hollywood as a script writer. He and Frank Crowninshield each wrote letters to their Hollywood friends like Sam Goldwyn, Gene Markey, director Frank Tuttle and other prominent movie people, all of whom replied that they would be happy to help me. Sam Jaffe, a well-known Hollywood agent, also wrote, asking if he could represent me. Armed with these promising letters ("I have been a fan of hers for some time and I shall be delighted to do anything I can for her"—Frank Tuttle; "I will do all I possibly can for her"—Sam Goldwyn), I set off by ship, bound for California via the Panama Canal. The ship made a stop at Havana, my favorite city, with the result that I never did get to Hollywood, thus thumbing my nose at yet another opportunity anyone with an ounce of ambition would have broken an arm to seize.

I stayed five months in Cuba. Back in New York, I turned down several offers of editorial jobs, including one which would have made me the only woman editor on the new picture magazine *Life*, then in preparation. I finally accepted a position as literary editor of *Harper's Bazaar*, but on the day I was due to report for work I sailed for Europe to visit Baruch, who was in Badgastein, Austria, recuperating from a gout attack. The lively *Vanity*

Fair years, when I was virtually my own boss, had spoiled me. I never wanted to work in any conventional office, a fate I managed to avoid for the next twenty-six years. I had sold my first free-lance effort, *Latins Are Lousy Lovers*, to *Esquire*. I mailed it to them on my own initiative, addressing it to The Editor and enclosing a self-addressed stamped envelope. They bought it for $125. I'm sure neither the editors nor I dreamed that I would become their champion contributor. To date, I have had seventy articles printed there, more than any other writer in the history of the magazine, with the exception of their regular monthly columnists. I also wrote for various other magazines, ranging from *Vogue, Town & Country, Harper's, Glamour* and *Mademoiselle* to less prestigious publications with names like *Pic, Click, Why, Dude, Swank, Nugget*. My articles have been published in forty-seven national magazines, including many now defunct, like *Look, Holiday, Pageant, Coronet, Collier's*. My work has been reprinted in eighteen countries (I was big for a while in Finland). My idea has always been to do the minimum amount of writing necessary in order to support myself and various members of my family. Fame has not been the spur. Rather, you might say, it was the neighborhood grocer.

Aside from newspapers and *Vanity Fair*, the two jobs I've most enjoyed were ones I did for free: shepherding a black Cuban voodoo troupe and helping to start a famous nightclub, Café Society Downtown. The voodoos came first.

Chapter Seven

VOODOO GODMOTHER

When I lived in Cuba my favorite night spot was Las Fritas, some distance outside Havana, a row of small bars and dancehalls, the best of which was Los Tres Hermanos, where the revelry lasted until after dawn, the patrons were mostly black, the music ranked with the best in Cuba and the dancing was uninhibited and marvelous. I went there so often that the performers all knew me and welcomed me with an enthusiasm probably not unconnected with the fact that my friends and I bought them all the rum they could drink, which was plenty.

Brujería, or witchcraft, had been banned in the country, although it still existed illegally. I was once taken to a *ñañigo,* or voodoo, ceremony in Regla, across the bay from Havana, where I was the only white person present. It was a scary experience and I squeamishly left during the ritual chicken sacrifice. Some of the Las Fritas groups took part in *ñañigo* rites, but always in secret. Their public performances were a sensual pastiche of pseudo-voodoo, exciting to watch, even though not the real thing. When the head of Crowell Publishing Company, who owned *Collier's,* visited Cuba he was taken to Los Tres Hermanos by an enterprising young woman who correctly calculated that he would be enthralled. She persuaded him that he should import a group of performers to New York as entertainers at the annual banquet his company gave for their advertisers. He posted bond for them, paid all expenses, and a troupe of seven—two dancers and five musicians—duly arrived in New York with the young woman as their den mother, who, not so incidentally, took charge of all the money. After they appeared at the banquet, she rented them out for appearances at a few private parties given by such groups as automobile executives, baseball magnates, Manhattan socialites and the Associated Cycle Trades of America. Then she vamoosed, leaving the voodoos almost penniless, speaking no English, friendless and stranded at the Dewey Square Hotel in Harlem, where she had stashed them and then left without paying their bill. She also neglected to give them their return fare to Cuba.

I was the only person they knew. I had met their transient impresario in Havana, so she looked me up after she arrived with the troupe in New York. Together, we gave a party, featuring the voodoos, at the Café Latino, a Greenwich Village nightclub owned by a Chilean friend of mine. The previous attraction there was the Peruvian singer Yma Sumac and her three male musicians. (Naturally, we nicknamed them the Four Inca Spots.) Yma's specialty was her ability to hit, and hold, the highest note of any singer in history, a record still unrivaled. She was a tough act to follow, but the voodoos were the answer. I sent invitations to columnists, magazine editors and people I knew in the entertainment world. No one had seen anything like them, and they were a sensation. Then, without warning, their den mother left town. Bewildered and panicky, they turned to me as their one friend. I didn't know what to do with them but I couldn't abandon them.

I spent the next week shuttling between my apartment and the Dewey Square Hotel. It was winter and when the voodoos saw their breath smoking in the air they were terrified and rushed back indoors to concoct a countermagic. At the first snowfall, they got up at five o'clock in the morning and went out to dance in the streets to ward off the evil spirit. They all caught colds, they were constipated and they suspiciously refused any medicine. I got around this by giving them Feen-A-Mint and telling them it was nice American gum. They chewed like mad and soon they felt better. But I couldn't fool them that way twice. They switched to *brujería* charms, super-special incantations and herbs sent them from Cuba by their mothers. Meanwhile, I persuaded Jim

Moriarity, a bright, witty, attractive man who ran the fashionable
Club Bali, to give them a booking and advance the money to bail
them out of their hotel. I also found them a theatrical agent, a
Miss Freeman. We moved the troupe to a small Harlem flat
which they decorated with pictures of St. Lazarus and the black
Santa Barbara, in front of which they kept lighted candles and
glasses filled with what they said were magic potions. Carmita, the
lone girl voodoo, made their costumes, cooked huge meals of
black beans and rice and read out loud to them from Spanish
comic books, which they called *muñequitos* (little dolls).

Once in a while they went to the movies. Or, to be more exact,
they went to one movie. They saw Kay Francis in *One Way Passage*
six times. Otherwise, they kept to themselves. None of them
had ever been inside a church and they didn't know that their
ñañigo cult was a mixture of Christianity, Masonic rites and African voodoo ceremonies. Their club performance was vibrant with
an almost violent sexuality, yet they were primly shocked by
Harlem night life. When not at work, they seldom budged from
their flat, where they always seemed to be celebrating a birthday
or the Saint's Day of one or another of them, or of their parents
or other relatives back home. They would sing and dance and
make music until way past sunrise, meanwhile drinking vast quan-
tities of something they called "*arráncame la vida*" ("tear my life
from me"), which was, quite simply, raw alcohol, sugar and a little lemon. Miss Freeman and her mother, who traveled in tan-
dem, were expected to attend these festivities, along with me, all
of us bearing appropriate gifts.

There were two problems. The first was that I had to act as interpreter. The voodoos called me their *madrina*, or godmother,
and I was supposed to mediate in their domestic arrangements as
well as professional ones and to be on tap at any hour to do so.
Freeman and Freeman's mother spoke no word of Spanish, nor
did Moriarity. I was always the go-between, a position that
required a certain amount of tact, especially where Ugarte, the
drummer, was concerned. He was a ferocious-looking man, with a
temper to match. A big man, with tremendous muscles, he had a
habitual air of sullen savagery and could frighten people with his
eyes. He and Freeman were frequently at loggerheads. When she
booked the troupe for parties in private homes, he was always spit-

ting on the rugs or going in the bathroom and using perfume, bril-
liantine, whatever he could find, and, on one occasion, drinking
an entire bottle of the hostess's expensive J. Floris rosewater
mouthwash. In another Park Avenue apartment he tried to open
a door to the room where he had left his drum. It didn't open immediately, so he leaned against it quickly with one massive shoul-
der and the door splintered into bits. His big dream was to get
Freeman to buy him some teeth—he had almost none—and her
repeated refusal drove him into such sulks that he would sometimes precipitate a crisis at the club. It was then that my diplomacy as interpreter came in handy. "You tell that fat bitch with a
face like a mango that I'm not appearing tonight until she prom-
ises to buy me my teeth." I translated this as, "He says that he's
deeply sorry but he is in such pain he fears he cannot perform. He
has problems in eating because he has no teeth." "You tell that
black bastard," Freeman said tartly, "that if he doesn't get his ass
out there and start beating his drum, I'll have him deported, teeth
or no teeth." In my translation this became, "Miss Freeman says
that you are such a great artist that your fame has spread far and
wide. The club is filled with people who have come to hear and
admire you. It is not fair to them to disappoint them." Eventually, with the promise of an extra bottle of rum, I would settle
the dispute and the show would go on.

The second problem was that someone had to introduce their
act, explaining the symbolism of the dances. There was no one
else available, so I was drafted. I had a supply of evening gowns
from my posh Condé Nast period, so, suitably attired and
fortified with some stiff drinks, I made a nightly appearance,
giving my little speech and ending with the command *"Empieza!"*
("Begin!"). *Variety* referred to me as a "class spieler," and my
friends thought it a terrific lark. The voodoos became the rage
of New York, written about by all the columnists, their pictures in the glossy magazines. The Club Bali leaflet for March
1937, edited by publicist Chic Farmer, listed among that month's
patrons Medora Roosevelt of the Oyster Bay Roosevelts, Mr.
and Mrs. Henry Mellon, Jr., Dashiell Hammett, Mark Hellinger
with his wife, the ex-Follies beauty Gladys Glad, Governor Frank
Murphy of Michigan (later Supreme Court justice), Herbert

Swope, Jr., a covey of Vanderbilts, and Pat O'Brian from Holly-wood.

Others who often came to see the troupe were Vincent Bendix, Constance Bennett, George Jean Nathan, Tullio Carminati, Ken-esaw Mountain Landis, Condé Nast, Princess Alice Rospigliosi, Cole Porter, Norman Bel Geddes. They were a must for students down from Yale, Harvard, Princeton, but their most devoted fans were other musicians. The star attraction was Ugarte's drum solo. He had never had a music lesson in his life but he was a magnificent drummer, beating with his hands on the big bongo drum made of animal skin. Gene Krupa and other drummers used to listen with awe to his masterly, spine-tingling performance. They came back again and again.

After two months at the Club Bali we all moved to Le Mirage —the voodoos, me, Freeman, Freeman's mother. I became a grad-ual dropout, although I remained, when necessary, their inter-preter, godmother and confidante. One day, Ugarte reproached me for not showing up at the club. "You should have seen me last night," he said. "I was phenomenal. There was some actress there who was crazy about me. She had me come to her table. She asked if I wanted a drink. I said, 'Sure. But you have to buy the others a drink, too.' She told me I was the most fantastic musician she had ever heard." I asked who she was. He shrugged. "What did she look like?" "She had a white face, white as the moon, and yellow hair. One eyebrow went way up this way—*zing!* The other went *that* way—*zoop!* And her eyelashes!" He made little horns of his fingers and waggled them in front of his eyes. "Señora, you may think that I lie, but if I am not telling you the truth I hope I get a telegram tomorrow that my mother is dead. Her eyelashes went way out to *here!*" That night the club press agent came to my table. "Did you hear about the drummer and Marlene Die-trich?" he asked.

It all ended when the voodoos decided they could not face an-other winter in New York. Also, they were homesick. They went back to Cuba for good, back to Las Fritas. It was twenty-two years before I saw them again. In 1959 I took my children to Havana and we spent an evening at Las Fritas, where we were welcomed with warm embraces. Ugarte let my young son play his bongo drum, and he danced with my daughter. He had learned a little

English. "How your mama?" he asked me. "She nice lady." "Does *he* know Granny?!" my daughter exclaimed incredulously. Yes, he did. I had taken all the voodoos to my mother's for dinner one Sunday when they were first dumped on me in New York.

I saw a couple of them one more time, in the summer of 1961, when I went to Cuba to do a feature for *Show* magazine. Ugarte hadn't changed one whit, in appearance or manners. "Did you bring me a present?" he demanded. "It is the custom, as you know." I gave him four cakes of soap I had swiped from my Miami hotel, and he went away happy.

Chapter Eight

CAFÉ SOCIETY DOWNTOWN

New Year's Eve, 1938, a basement on Sheridan Square, in Greenwich Village opened its door to the public and became a landmark in American nightclub history. The name was Café Society, later amended to Café Society Downtown. It was our first political nightclub. Jazz and politics were what it was all about. Some people hated it; others were all agog. It was the most exciting night spot in town and the proving ground for more remarkable talent than possibly any similar place before or since. It was where Billie Holiday, Hazel Scott, Lena Horne, Josh White, Meade-Lux Lewis, Albert Ammons, Joe Turner, Pete Johnson, Teddy Wilson, Frankie Newton, Hot Lips Page and others of that caliber got their start. I don't mean it was the first job any of them had, but it was what made them famous.

So what's newsworthy about this now? God knows it's been written about before. Doesn't everyone know all about it? Not quite. What everybody doesn't know is that the club was founded to raise money for the Communist Party.

I helped to start it; I gave it its name; I did all the early publicity and wrote the advertisements; I auditioned a few of the performers; and for the first months I acted as unofficial hostess, sort of a B-girl de luxe. I did it all for no pay and I loved every minute. I suppose not everyone connected with the club, and certainly not all the customers, knew of the political link. I am sure the waiters, as well as many of the entertainers, were ignorant of it. Few people, however, could have been utterly unaware of the left-wing ambiance. After all, the slogan I coined, which was printed on our matchbooks and used in our ads, was "The wrong place for the Right people."

I spent the summer of 1938 in South America, ostensibly gathering material for travel articles for *Vogue, Harper's Bazaar* and *Town & Country*, but actually doing a secret survey of the underground movement against brutal military dictatorships, as well as an analysis of the political situation created by fascist penetration of the continent by the Axis powers, Germany, Italy and Japan. When I returned, I wrote a report on the latter for Bernard Baruch, who gave it to Cordell Hull, the Secretary of State. My report on the underground resistance movement was given orally to Earl Browder, then head of the American Communist Party, who came to see me in my one-room Greenwich Village flat. Although I was not a Party member, I was sympathetic and what in those days was called a fellow traveler. That was the decade of the Depression, the Spanish Civil War, Fascism in Italy, Hitler and the Nazis in Germany. I think it was John O'Hara who remarked that during that time "all the best people followed the Party line." They were later to be referred to as premature antifascists.

However, the relevant point here is that I saw Browder a second time, when he told me of the plans for a nightclub and asked if I would help. Some friends of mine were already involved in setting it up. Through them I met Barney Josephson, a shoe salesman from New Jersey, who was to run the club. It is possible that the club was his idea in the first place. Certainly, he was the legal owner, although he has said in interviews that the shoe business failed during the Depression and that he came to New York with only $7.80. I don't know the financial details, but enough money was found to rent for $200 a month the basement at 2 Sheridan Square and to finance the business of getting it together. Barney knew nothing about operating a nightclub, but he learned, although not without assistance from the rest of us eager beavers, most of whom worked gratis. A group of well-known artists, including Adolph Dehn, Anton Refregier, Syd Hoff, John Groth, William Gropper, Ad Reinhardt, Sam Berman and Abe Birnbaum, painted the witty murals that gave the club its distinctive decor, a far cry from the flossy banality of uptown night spots.

The person most responsible for the club's success was John Hammond, Jr., a crew-cut young man still in his twenties, who found us the musical talent that was to become legendary. Hammond was mad about Negro music: blues and boogie-woogie, not Uncle Tom spirituals or furrowed-brow intellectual jazz, but the black gutbucket music from the whorehouses, honky-tonks and gin mills of New Orleans, Chicago, Kansas City. He was in charge of all hot jazz for a couple of recording companies, but he also had an office at the *People's Press*, a weekly labor newspaper he helped support. Someone went to see him. I don't know what he was told about the club, except that it would feature the kind of music he loved best. He became enthusiastic and he scoured the country, searching for what he wanted. He found Meade-Lux Lewis washing cars in a Chicago garage. Albert Ammons, who had taught himself music by putting nickels in a player piano and then following the keys, was driving a Chicago taxi. Together, they formed the greatest-ever duo of boogie-woogie pianists, their place in the hagiography of twentieth-century hot music forever luminous.

No one had heard of Billie Holiday except Hammond, who first heard her singing in an obscure dump and knew she was the greatest thing since Bessie Smith. He located the veteran blues singer Ida Cox in a black burlesque house in Jersey City. Lena Horne had made it as far as the Paramount movie theater on Broadway, where she was singing with Charlie Barnet's band, but Hammond made her a star by bringing her downtown to Café Society. He brought the great blues shouter Joe Turner and the pianist Pete Johnson from what might be termed the lower depths of Kansas City. His taste was infallible. It was what made the club.

None of us could think of a suitable name for the place. Every suggestion was immediately shot down. The original plan was to satirize uptown café society, the people who today would be called the jet set. Rather idly, I said, "I suppose we could call it just that—Café Society." I didn't think it was a brilliant idea but the others liked it, so it was settled. Barney always told interviewers that the name was suggesed by Clare Boothe Luce, probably because he figured, rightly, that her name was more news-worthy than mine. I did tell her about the club, without mentioning the political affiliation, but she had nothing to do with it. She was only in the place once, as my guest, and she certainly did not name it, although by now I wouldn't be surprised if she thinks she did. In fact, the first recording of "Café Society Rag" by Joe Turner and Pete Johnson contained the line "Helen Norden give it its lovely name." In later recordings, the line was expunged, but I still have my old 78, or did until someone sat on it. It's a collector's item now. I recently met a man who has one and he promised to have a tape made of it for me.

Because we were supposed to parody the fashionable uptown clubs I wanted to have our cigarette girl wander around chanting "Cigars, cigarettes, wolfhounds," and I called a meeting of the waiters and told them to insult the patrons. "For example," I instructed, "say to women, 'What an awful hat!' If someone asks, 'How is the veal?' you answer, 'Terrible.' Spill a little water on the table and then say, 'Wipe it up yourself.'" I was full of similarly jolly suggestions and the waiters, to a man, were appalled. They said they simply couldn't do it, so I abandoned the idea. (A few years later, two men opened an uptown club based on the same scheme, where the customers were mercilessly ribbed and insulted. It was a big success.)

We opened with Frankie Newton's six-man band, Frankie playing his trumpet. Teddy Wilson played piano, Billie Holiday sang, and Jack Gilford, a wonderfully funny comedian, was our master of ceremonies, as well as doing his own act. We were an immediate hit and the place was jammed every night. From the beginning, it was completely integrated: black and white performers, black and white patrons. This had never happened before, outside of a few Harlem places where the whites got the best tables. Not at Café Society they didn't! We had absolutely no color bar, no preferential treatment. We often had indignant patrons walk out, not only because of our black patrons but sometimes because of the political content of the songs and monologues. Zero Mostel, who had been living in a loft and working on a WPA art project, had his first professional engagement with us, at forty dollars a week. His satiric monologue as Senator Polltax P. Pellagra did not endear him to many of our southern white guests. Nor did Billie

Holiday's nightly singing of "Strange Fruit," that haunting song in which the "strange fruit" were the lynched bodies of black men hanging from southern trees. Lights were turned out, except for one small spot on Billie's face, and all table service was stopped. When the last acrid words were sung in that bittersweet whine, there was always a momentary tribute of silence, as people sat stunned and shaken.

The film about Billie, *Lady Sings the Blues*, was a slick and evasive Hollywood job. Diana Ross, with her false eyelashes and pretty face, was not Billie, any more than her polished Motown voice was Billie's. Ethel Waters said that Billie sang as if her shoes were too tight. Her voice had a plangent moan, sometimes harsh, sometimes thin, always mesmeric. No beauty, she used little make-up and was somewhat on the plump side, although in later years she learned to fix herself up more. In her Café Society days no one would have given her a second look, until she began to sing. Then, the combination of despair and hatred in her tone was heart-rending. Even her happier songs had a tinge of something strange and penetrating, something of "a woman wailing for her demon lover."

Her life was a tough and seamy one. Born in Baltimore to a thirteen-year-old mother and a fifteen-year-old father, who were married when Billie was three, she was running errands at the age of six for the madam of a local brothel. She spent some time in reform school and was a prostitute in New York at thirteen. She was about twenty-three when she started singing at Café Society. There were people who came night after night just to hear her. She had many devoted admirers from the theatrical world, and at one period there was a rich white girl, obviously fascinated by her, who used to take her home with her after the show. Billie wasn't easy to know. Moody and withdrawn, she seemed indifferent to her success. Barney has said that she wasn't a junkie when she was working for the club. I wouldn't be quite sure about that. In the years after she left us, she was busted three times on heroin charges, went to prison on one of the raps, and was barred from singing in New York clubs, bars or cabarets. Her first husband had turned her on to opium. I'm talking about hard drugs, not something harmless like marijuana, which she had been smoking since she was a teen-ager. This was nothing. A lot of us did in the Thirties, although Barney, who was puritanical in that inflexible style of many old-time Lefties, insisted that anyone caught smoking in his club would be fired on the spot. Just the same, I could often detect in the ladies' room the unmistakable smell of what we then called reefers, and the musicians used to share a joint in the men's room, spraying cologne around to disguise the odor in case Barney should pop in.

I sent items about the club to all the columnists and entertainment editors, most of whom I knew at the time, or at least they knew about me and had often mentioned me in my Condé Nast days. The publicity was so extensive that I had an offer from the Plaza Hotel to become their press agent, but I politely declined. I even had an article in *Vogue*, written while we were still getting the club ready, which appeared on the stands the day after our opening. It was a general piece about how to run a nightclub, pointing out that gangster backing was usually an indispensable requisite and that good liquor had nothing to do with success because I knew clubs where the drinks were so bad they were practically Mickey Finns, yet the tables were crowded and customers stood five deep at the bar. The formula for success in big Broadway clubs was nude girls, or as near nude as permissible in those days. The International Casino, a mecca for out-of-town tourists and businessmen on a spree, always featured a display of aphrodisiac young flesh draped with sequins, feathers, spangles. Their P.R. man pointed out to me that the girls were all foreigners, apparently because it seemed to be more titillating to know that you were looking at a nude Finnish girl than at one from Schenectady. In the fashionable Upper East Side *boîtes*, the main attraction was the sight of celebrities, wined and dined free of charge because they served as bait for other customers. Every smart uptown club had a snob appeal free list and it was startling to discover the number of glamorous Social Registerites who would go out and get drunk night after night without paying a cent, happy in the knowledge that ordinary people were paying to come and stare at them.

The main point of my article and the only reason I wrote it was to tell about the new nightclub about to open, Café Society in Greenwich Village, which would flout all these traditional recipes for success by having good liquor, great entertainment, no gangsters, no nude girls, no café society free list. In fact, the idea of the new place was that it would be a satire on other clubs like the old El Morocco and the Stork, from the decorations to the floor show, and its aim and purpose were to spoof the café society people of uptown.

The article was widely read and the result was that those very people I attacked started flocking to our club to see for themselves what was going on. Thus, on some nights we would have ex-debutante Brenda Frazier and friends sitting next to a table of longshoremen (a former rank-and-file longshoreman was Barney's assistant and in charge of the bartenders) or officials from the more progressive trade unions almost cheek by jowl with heads of companies in whose factories their members worked. Our most consistent patrons, however, were people like Budd Schulberg, Lionel Stander, Paul Robeson, Mrs. Eleanor Roosevelt, Lillian Hellman, S. J. Perelman, St. Clair McKelway. I was doing my hostess act one night at a table with several writers when one of them spotted a blond of Rubenesque proportions who had been hanging out at the bar. He left our table and approached her, only to have her flee from his approaches like some out-size dryad frightened by Pan. He pursued her from one corner of the club to another until she took refuge in the ladies' room. I went in there and found her in a fine fury. "But that's one of our most famous humorists," I said soothingly. "Some humorist!" she snorted. "He kept calling me 'earth mother' and saying he wanted to pour his hot sperm into me. I told him he can keep his old hot sperm. I don't want it."

We made some mistakes but not many. Barney once hired, on his own, a couple of midgets who did ballroom dancing, the man in white tie and tails, the woman in long evening dress. I am not against midgets per se. It was just that their wedding cake figurine cuteness simply did not fit the rest of the club. A couple of us issued an ultimatum to Barney: "Those midgets have got to go." They went. Another time, my friend Renee and I auditioned a pair whose sophisticated routine had been a hit in uptown spots. We persuaded Barney to hire them. They didn't fit in, either. Then there was the time that I, all alone, auditioned Hazel Scott and turned her down. Jack Gilford had heard her singing and playing piano in a Harlem bar. He persuaded Barney to go to hear her and she was hired for $65 a week. She was eighteen, not particularly good-looking but a great swing pianist, although Hammond never really liked her. She worked for Barney for seven years and turned down an offer from the Waldorf-Astoria of $1,000 a week, a lot more than Barney was paying. She said Barney had given her her first break and besides, she liked the club because it was a place where she could bring her friends. Years later, when she married Congressman Adam Clayton Powell, it was Barney who gave the bride away.

When Lena Horne worked at the club she was known as Helena Horne. Hammond brought her there when I was away for a month, visiting friends in South Carolina. When I returned, I was told, "There's a new singer at the club who looks like your mother." We went to hear her and I was surprised at the resemblance. It was like looking at my mother as I remembered her when she was in her twenties. The similarity could have been due to the Indian blood in both women. Helena had long black hair hanging below her shoulders and a sort of old-fashioned classic face. This was before Hollywood make-up men glamourized her and made her into the ravishing beauty she became. It was also before she adopted some of the theatrical grimaces and mannerisms that often seem an obligatory stylistic routine for famous women singers not content to leave well enough alone but determined to enhance their act by unnecessary affectations.

My club favorites were Joe Turner, the blues shouter, and Pete Johnson, the pianist. I publicized them as "Big Joe Turner from Kansas City" and "Roll 'em Pete Johnson." They were both sensational and Joe, in particular, was a magnet for women. On one occasion this resulted in an internecine hassle. Among our dedicated patrons were two Hollywood script writers whom we nicknamed Tisket and Tasket. They both had Mexican wives. Tisket's wife, Josephine, had been an itinerant fruit picker in California. She was strikingly handsome, but it was the other wife, Raquel, who caused the ruckus. She used to work in a bawdy house in Los Angeles, and she was one of the most exquisitely pretty girls I've ever seen. She had a quiet voice and a gentle, dignified manner. These qualities, together with her really astounding beauty—she looked like a young Dolores Del Rio—naturally made a good impression on her clients. It was commonly reported that Dashiell

Hammett once rented her out for a week, like a library book, and took her home with him. Her script writer husband met her at her place of work, fell in love with her, and they were married.

When Tisket and Tasket returned to Hollywood for script jobs, their wives remained in New York and were nightly visitors at the club. Like the rest of us girls, Raquel was attracted to Big Joe Turner. She found out that when the club closed, he and Pete Johnson usually went to an after-hours place in Harlem. She asked me to find out where. In the ladies' room I asked Hazel Scott, but she snubbed me. "I don't know any places like that in Harlem," she said haughtily. "I live with my mother and I never go out." Raquel found out anyway, and the next development was that a few weeks later Barney came into the club livid with rage. It seemed that Raquel had gone to bed with Joe and couldn't resist telling Josephine. The latter informed her husband, who felt it his duty to report to Raquel's husband, and the fat was in the fire. What made it ironic was that these were all people with strong left-wing sympathies, if not actual affiliations. They were staunch fighters for integration, but apparently not to the extent of integration at home. Barney was beside himself with anger. He sent for Joe to come to his office. I felt I had to give Joe warning, so that he wouldn't be caught off guard. He was in the men's room, but I scribbled a quick note: "Barney knows about you and Raquel. He's mad as hops." I gave it to one of the musicians who was standing outside the men's room. "Give this to Joe immediately," I said. It was just in the nick of time. Joe told me afterward that while Barney was storming at him and denouncing him, he kept thinking of one of Jack Gilford's monologues, a parody on murder mysteries. "Barney's yellin' away at me and I kept sayin', 'No sir, I didn't do it,' but all the time I kept wantin' to say, 'The butler did it. The butler did it.'"

Barney fired Joe. My friend Renee and her husband and I went to Barney and we quit. After all, the slogan was "Black and white, Unite and fight." Barney took him back again, but then he received a letter from Raquel's husband, demanding that Joe be fired permanently, so the battle was on again. As Joe said to me, "I never did see so much hell over one woman gettin' fucked."

All of us, including Joe, insisted to Barney that Raquel made the whole thing up. I knew differently. I had been to the after-hours place, an apartment in Harlem, with Joe, and the woman who ran the place told me the story. "That Raquel, she just wouldn't leave poor Joe alone. She kept after him and he kept turnin' her away. Then one night she come out stark naked, with just a little maid's apron tied round her waist. She sat on Joe's lap and put her arms round him and begun kissin' him. He's only human. What was he supposed to do, fight her off?"

We finally prevailed on Barney to keep Joe. He did it reluctantly, probably only because Joe was one of the club's major attractions. I took Raymond Moley and Ralph Robey one night to hear him. Moley, a former Columbia law professor and ex-Assistant Secretary of State, had been the head of President Franklin Roosevelt's famous Brain Trust. He coined the phrase New Deal and was once called "the second strongest man in Washington." Cordell Hull disliked him because Moley got too big for his boots and by-passed Hull, his superior, on several matters, acts that brought about a rupture with Roosevelt. Moley resigned from the government in 1933 and went to work for Vincent Astor, part owner of *Newsweek,* for which Moley wrote a political column for thirty years.

Robey, a former vice-president and chief economist of the National Association of Manufacturers, was *Newsweek*'s financial expert. His rather unusual hobby was knitting glass hats. I never saw one so I don't know how he did it, or why, although I do remember that around that time an unsuccessful attempt was made to popularize men's suits made of glass in Italy. I had some white kitchen window curtains made of glass fiber, so I suppose it was the same process, except Robey knitted his hats by hand.

It also turned out that he was crazy about gutbucket music. I met both men at a dinner at Baruch's. As we left, they asked me to have drinks with them and took me to the St. Regis. When I told them about Café Society, Robey insisted that we go there. The St. Regis elevator was crowded. Soon, we were all sniffing in a baffled way. There was an oddly pungent odor. What could it be? I put my hand in one pocket of my jacket, searching for a handkerchief. The pocket was filled with mothballs. I quickly explored the other pocket. More mothballs. It was a black skunk fur jacket which I had left at my mother's house the preceding summer, instead of putting it in storage. I should have known better. My mother was a mothball addict. She put them in everything every spring—blankets, suits, sweaters, to keep away moths; linen towels, tablecloths, napkins, to repel mice; flower beds to discourage cats from peeing there. She even stuck them in the corners of sofas and upholstered armchairs because someone told her that if the dog got fleas they would jump onto the furniture and breed, but mothballs would prevent this. I hadn't lived at home for so long that I had forgotten this annual routine. So there I was, squeezed into the St. Regis elevator, my pockets filled with mothballs. I suppose it was the body heat in the packed elevator that brought out the scent which overpowered the expensive Chanel, Guerlain and Lanvin perfumes worn by the other women.

I remained silent until we hit the street. Then I went to the curb and emptied my pockets while Moley and Robey watched in amazement. I didn't even bother to explain, so I guess they probably thought I always carried them around in case I ran into a swarm of moths. By the time we reached Café Society, we had forgotten about it, anyway. Robey loved the club, especially Joe Turner and Pete Johnson. Moley was more interested in drinking. He began to get maudlin and told me his life history. His father was a tailor. "He worked with his hands," he kept repeating reverently, as if that were some sort of proletarian kudo. "I don't want to be a reactionary," he said, putting his hand on my knee. "You can save me!" It could be called one of the lesser romantic approaches.

I introduced them to Joe and Pete and when the club closed we five went to Harlem together to the after-hours apartment. We all had a lot more to drink. Pete played the piano and Joe sang—an incredible, explosive performance. They were always exciting at the club, but here, home in Harlem, they outdid themselves, simply for their own pleasure. It was an electrifying experience to hear them. Moley was too drunk to enjoy it and he disappeared into one of the bedrooms with a black girl he picked up at the bar, but Robey and I sat enthralled. I wanted it to last forever. It was already midmorning when Robey remembered he had to give a lecture. He left. I kissed Joe good night and collected Moley. When our taxi stopped at the St. Regis, where he lived at a discount rate, courtesy of Vincent Astor, he tried to get me to go to his room. "Sorry," I said, "but you're no competition for Big Joe

Turner." He was furious. "After all the money I've spent on you tonight!" he exclaimed petulantly, apparently forgetting the black girl and also that Robey had paid at least half the bills. "I'll send you a check tomorrow," I said, as I pushed him gently out the taxi door and gave the driver my address. "Where'd you get them two sad-ass ofays, honey?" Joe asked me that night at the club. I didn't explain to him about the Brain Trust. He thought all white folks were crazy enough, anyway.

Gradually, I began to drop away from the club. I was in love with Jack Lawrenson and after our marriage we continued to go there, but only as customers. A paid publicist, Ivan Black, was hired to replace me and I handed over to him my impressive publicity scrapbook, which probably helped make his job easier for him. A couple of years later, Barney opened Café Society Uptown, on the Upper East Side. It was successful, but it never had the same ambiance as the downtown club. Barney made money and sold both places around 1950, when newspapers began to attack both clubs as "Red." I think this came about because of the publicity connected with Barney's brother, Leon Josephson, a lawyer, who was often in the downtown club. He was a far more attractive man than Barney. Barney always reminded me of some kind of albino rodent, with his thin white hair, pasty complexion, pink-rimmed eyes. I don't really mean this in an unpleasant sense. It's just that he struck me as mousy, or perhaps rabbity, but not in a cuddly way. Leon was tall and much better-looking, with a quiet sense of humor. An admitted Communist, he was subpoenaed by the Un-American Activities Committee in 1948. He refused to answer questions and was sent to prison for contempt. The case was covered in the papers and the reputation of the two clubs suffered as a result. However, Barney had enough money to start The Cookery restaurants. He has never publicly admitted any left-wing affiliation, although his sympathies could not be denied. His first wife, Isabel, once told me that he used to read out loud to her every night in bed from the *History of the Communist Party of the Soviet Union*, a huge volume of impenetrable prose. She said it was agonizingly boring. Poor Isabel. Maybe Barney was just trying to find out what it was all about. Maybe.

In June 1973 the Newport Jazz Festival organizers gave a "Salute to Café Society" at Carnegie Hall. Barney was presented with a plaque as a tribute for his having fostered the careers of the many famous musicians, singers and entertainers who worked in both the Café Society clubs. I suppose he did, in a way, but he didn't "discover" any of them. The plaque should have gone to John Hammond. Be that as it may, Barney Josephson's name is now recorded in the annals of jazz music as one of its great benefactors. He has his plaque to prove it. Maybe it should have been the Order of Lenin.

Chapter Nine

THERE'S A RED IN MY BED AND IT'S ME

Most ex-Communists and former fellow travelers can say, usually defensively, that they were ideological victims of the Thirties. In those years of the Depression, the Spanish Civil War, Fascists and Nazis, the Party seemed to them to be on the side of the angels. The implication is that they would never have been attracted had it not been for the historical situation at that time.

I am sure this is correct for many of these people, some of whom became more speedy apostates than others, thus casting a shadow of doubt on the integrity of their original interest. They wouldn't put it this way. They would say that their eyes were at last opened. According to them, they had been duped, hoodwinked, bamboozled, misled. Apparently, never in our history have there been so many intelligent people going around with their eyes shut, imbecilely ductile, intellectually unable to tell ass from elbow. Hmmm. God knows I myself have been disillusioned by plenty of Communists but I do not cite as exculpation that they made a fool of me. It remains true that other Communists have been the finest people I have known in my life.

It's not Communism that's at fault for misdeeds. It's people. The fact that there are bad, even evil, Communists does not invalidate the theory of Communism, any more than the concept of Christianity is nullified by bad or evil Christians. The doctrine of the brotherhood of man was spelled out long before Marx. It has

always been anathema to those in power. Occupiers of the seats of
the mighty never vacate them willingly. To avoid having them
pulled out from under them, they have to convince the majority
of the people that those seeking to dislodge them are evil. This is
often done in the name of religion, as, for example, when Billy
Sunday, the most famous evangelist of post-World War I days,
hysterically denounced the idea of the brotherhood of man as
"the worst rot that was ever dug out of hell." I assume he was
referring to the dreaded Bolshevik menace and not to one of the
basic tenets of Christianity.

I do not have the excuse of the desperate Thirties for my own
initial sympathy with Communism, because it began in 1929, before the Wall Street crash, in that last year of the good old Herbert Hoover chicken-in-every-pot boom days. I have written elsewhere how I met my first Communist through my work as a
newspaper reporter in Syracuse. She was the most decent, intelligent, highly principled person I had ever known, and she is still
my friend. Previously, I didn't know what Communism was, not
even to the extent of regarding it as a bugaboo. I learned from my
friend and her associates, from the books and pamphlets they gave
me, from the cogency of their argument.

I didn't join the Party then because I had never joined anything. I was never a Girl Guide or a Girl Scout. There were no
sororities at Vassar and neither there nor previously at boarding
school did I become a member of any of the clubs such as Drama
Club, Pen Club, Glee Club. (Could it really have been called
such a silly name? Yes, it was. A Glee Club was a music club,
mostly singing. I couldn't carry a tune so that would have been
out, anyway.) I belonged to no church group or political group or
hobby group, like bird watchers, or to the Junior League or the
DAR, for both of which I was eligible. In fact, it took me sixteen
years before I became a card-carrying Communist, and then I left
after less than a year.

Many people branded as Communists have stated that they
were never members. I believe this, because when I finally decided
to join, the man who was going to sign my card as sponsor realized that he himself had never joined, although he thought of
himself as a member and other people thought of him as one.
This turned out to be the case with several others who kept trying

to recruit me into the ranks. As a nonmember, it was true of me, too. I was instrumental in persuading other people to join; I marched in May Day parades; under the name of Mary O'Brian I wrote articles for the *Sunday Worker* (I was asked to become film critic for the *Daily Worker* but I refused); I raised money for various causes; I did political surveys for the Party hierarchy; I could have been seen as a rapt observer during at least one Communist Party national convention which I remember chiefly for the emotionally charged incident when about one hundred members of the crew of the *Île de France*, then in port, marched into the hall and down the aisle, fists clenched in the Communist salute, singing the Marseillaise and then the Internationale, while everyone stood in tribute.

Emotional fulfillment was a factor in the appeal of Communism for many—the songs, the slogans, the messianic spirit—and this sometimes slopped over into sentimentality. I knew women whose eyes filled with tears at the mere thought of "the workers," blissfully unaware that "the workers" can be just as reactionary, bigoted and cruel as their employers. For some, the Party was a way of belonging, a refuge from limbo. It gave them a sense of purpose and meaningful companionship. For others, it provided that unparalleled feeling of superiority that accompanies the conviction that one is doing something noble.

Then there were those who joined for the social life. I remember one girl who had marvelous eyes but, also, buck teeth and acne. Membership in the waterfront section of the Party gave her a popularity she had never known before, as well as prestige emanating from her job as a Condé Nast receptionist who actually saw in the flesh the rich, the famous, the talented of that era —because while working-class Party members might despise the assets of the upper bourgeoisie and the super-celebrities, they also tended to be as impressed by them as the rest of the population. The Party gave this girl self-confidence. It is worth noting that when she got better jobs, made money, had her teeth fixed and outgrew her acne, she stopped paying her dues, quit the Party and never wanted to see any of her old comrades, even to the point of cutting them cold if she happened to run into them.

Thus there were different kinds of motivation apart from dedication to social justice or the more practical urge to improve living standards, especially one's own. I myself didn't become a radical because of any personal poverty, oppression or exploitation. I became one, and I have remained one, because of intellectual conviction. I have no illusions about the fact that this has stopped considerably short of action. Communists are human beings and human beings are nothing if not fallible. I am never unduly surprised at the number of dropouts and renegades, whatever their reasons. When push comes to shove, it is not easy to be heroic. Besides, many Party members didn't join for socialist aims; they were planted for capitalist ones. Earl Browder's chauffeur and bodyguard, who was one of those who tried to persuade me to join (he used to take me dancing and once said, as he whirled me around the floor, "How do you like the way we recruit?"), cynically warned me that whenever three Communists were together, you could almost always figure that two were phony or would turn phony. Doubtless this was fanciful exaggeration, even though he adduced the case of one country where four out of six of the Party's Central Committee turned out to be spies. He also told me about a country in the Balkans where there was no Communist Party but there was a great deal of unrest among workers and peasants. To combat this, the government trained special police in Marxism and then sent them out to organize a Communist Party. In this way they got together the potential leaders of revolt, the possible militants. Once their Communist group was formed, the police then clapped them all in prison. This put paid to any more organized resistance to the status quo, or, as repressive governments always put it, "Order was restored."

The American Communist Party was notoriously infiltrated by informers, some working for the FBI, some for capitalist employers. At one time it used to be said that spies practically kept the Party going with their dues and contributions. Some of them acted as agents provocateurs but mostly they reported names of members and what went on at meetings. I remember being astonished by one episode during my brief membership in the cultural section. A strange man came into the meeting—I suppose he must have been known to someone there but most of us had never seen him before—and gave us all sheets of paper. He told us to write down the names of everybody we knew who might possibly be sympathetic to Party aims or interested in receiving Party

literature. This seemed to me to be a blatantly obvious bit of espi-
onage. I could have been wrong but I wasn't taking any chances
so I made up a few names and fake addresses. Afterward, when I
mentioned my suspicion, the others dismissed it as nonsense.
However, I am convinced that all the names written down went
on some FBI list.

It was in 1945 that I became an actual member. Our unit in the
cultural section was called the Ben Franklin Club, but if I were to
be hung up by my thumbs I could not remember where the meetings were held, except that I took the Sixth Avenue subway. The
group was a decidedly mixed bag: novelists, poets, beauty column
journalists, cookery writers, press agents, ghost writers, a playwright who seldom showed up, a couple of film script writers and
assorted journalistic odds and ends. The only really well known
member was Howard Fast, who later recanted. He dominated the
meetings and was openly contemptuous of those among us whom
he considered insignificant. Toward the end of my membership he
divided us into two groups: those he designated as real writers, of
whom he was the self-appointed leader, and a sort of catchall clus-
ter of the cookery and beauty writers and such. He put me in with
the latter, and we met separately. However, before this division
took place, I had some six months in which to observe the ludicrous inefficacy of the club. Very few of them had had any contact with workers and trade unionists or knew anything about
them. Their attitude was strictly elitist.

Two things stand out in my memory. One was Fast's snobbish
reference to Mike Gold, a well known, well loved and influential
Communist writer, author of *Jews Without Money*, whose simple,
straightforward style had great appeal for the working-class readers
to whom it was directed. Gold was not a member of our group—
probably had too much sense—and when someone mentioned his
name as a good example of an effective revolutionary propa-
gandist, Fast dismissed him by saying, "But he's such a bad
writer," as if *belles lettres* were what counted most. (After all,
Fast himself was no Thomas Mann.)

The other thing I remember was an entire meeting devoted to
long, rambling speeches about the function of the cultural section, summed up in a statement by one comrade: "What we really need is a magazine in which to experiment with new word

forms." This was at a time when the monstrous horror of our
atom bombs had stunned the world and when there were all the
problems of readjustment to the end of World War II, including
the conversion of war factories to peacetime manufacture. I was
astounded that this silly, frivolous suggestion about experimenting
with "new word forms" should be put forward as a serious Communist aim, but it was appreciatively received by most of the
other members present, who continued to discuss it.

The only constructive action of the Ben Franklin Club during
my membership was to campaign for Communist Ben Davis, a
Georgia-born Negro graduate of Amherst and Harvard Law
School. Davis had joined the Party in 1933, when he successfully
defended Angelo Herndon, a young black Communist who faced
the death penalty for leading an unemployment protest march in
Georgia. During the apocalyptic anti-Communist crusade of the
late Forties and early Fifties, Davis and eleven other Party leaders
were tried and convicted under the later to be repealed Smith
Act. He served three years and four months of a five-year sentence
in the federal prison at Terre Haute, Indiana. In 1959 he became
national secretary of the Party, a position he held until his death
in 1964. A genial, highly intelligent, cultured man, a chess expert
and an accomplished violinist, he was respected even by political
opponents, save for the most rabid.

He was elected to the New York City Council in 1943 and in
1945 he ran for re-election. Members of the Ben Franklin Club
were sent out in pairs to ring doorbells and try to get people to
pledge their votes. Most of the others were assigned to uptown
and midtown areas and to Greenwich Village, but my partner and
I got the Lower East Side. The slums and tenements we visited
were a revelation to me, as I hadn't known that there were people
in the great, rich city of New York who lived amid such filth and
misery. Most of the broken-down tenements had no toilets at all,
and cardboard boxes of excrement stood in the halls. We often
made our calls in the evening and I still remember the families on
Rivington Street sitting in total darkness because they didn't have
money for electric or gas lights. It was a sobering experience. For
the most part, people welcomed us, probably because they were
glad to have visitors, but I wouldn't want to speculate on how
many of them kept their pledges to vote for Davis. However, he

was elected, and I felt that I had at least taken a small part in something valid instead of sitting for hours listening to people talk about their own writing. In 1946 I simply stopped going to the meetings. I guess I wasn't missed, as no one ever contacted me about my dropout.

Most of my experience was with the waterfront section of the Party, although I never belonged to it. Merchant seamen and longshoremen, together with many of their womenfolk, were a different kettle of fish from the Ben Franklin Club. In fact, they were different from any of the other Communist groups. For one thing, some of them were in and out of the Party so often you would have thought the waterfront section had swinging doors. There was a time when many of the staunchest Communists either were expelled or had left of their own accord. Several went back in; others did not, although they remained Communists in thought and action.

For another thing, the seamen were generally of a rollicking, ribald nature. Although no less serious than other Communists, even their deepest convictions were often accompanied by a colorful vocabulary and a sense of humor notably lacking in more circumspect Party members. Thus, Blackie Myers, a vice-president of the National Maritime Union, could say to a union meeting that jeered at his support of a Party line proposal, "Go ahead and boo. I'm no first-time piecee," a reference familiar to seamen as the come-on of Asian prostitutes soliciting with the enticement, "Me first-time piecee." He then added, "If you think so, you've got bubbles in your think tank."

Paddy, a short, slightly cross-eyed Ulster Irishman, was waterfront section organizer. He had been a political commissar with the Abraham Lincoln Brigade in the Spanish Civil War, fighting against Franco. The rebel Fascists spread stories of atrocities supposedly committed by their enemies, including one that when government troops captured a village they hung all the nuns on meat hooks. This was ridiculous in view of the fact that the Republican soldiers were also Catholics, but it is a favorite propaganda piece in almost all wars and it is always believed, without any basis for proof. Paddy told about one small town they captured where he led his men into a convent and found all the terrified nuns cowering in a corner. "Don't worry, girls. You're

safe," he said, giving the nearest one a friendly pat on the fanny,
at which she let out a piercing shriek. It was only when he
presented them with a bottle of wine, some bread and cheese,
that he managed to calm their fears.

I was in section headquarters once when several members were
discussing women. "Puerto Rican girls are flighty," one man
solemnly announced. "Tut, tut, comrade," Paddy said. "That is a
chauvinist statement. I could have you defrocked for that." Aside,
he said to me, "We like our trade unions vertical and our women
horizontal." In general, though, anyone who joined the Party with
the hope of a sexual free-for-all was due for a shock. "Free love?"
one man said to me. "There's *nothing* free in the Party! Every
time I say hello to a Communist it costs me money." This was
true. The comrades were constantly and persistently selling literature and raffle tickets, collecting money for myriad worthy causes,
giving fund-raising parties. Even when they asked you to sign a pe-
tition, they frequently requested a contribution, too. There was
no "Moscow gold." The Party was entirely supported by rank-and-
file members, sympathizers, and what they could manage to
collect.

The waterfront section was rather conspicuously devoid of the
puritanism that characterized many other groups. There was quite
a bit of bedding that went on, as was only natural for sailors who
had a more cosmopolitan attitude toward sex. This was not always
appreciated by other Party functionaries, one of whom, delivering
a lecture to the waterfront section on the equality of women, was
dumbfounded to be greeted with guffaws when he exhorted his
audience, "We must push the women up from behind!"

We spent a lot of time going to What's Ons. These were fund-
raising parties listed in the *Daily Worker* under the heading of
What's On. They ranged from small social gatherings in people's
homes to lectures, dances, concerts and discussion groups, all with
admission fees and usually a collection as well. Some of the parties were attended by sympathetic uptown socialites or theater
and film celebrities or other entertainers. At one party in a Village
apartment in 1934 the star attraction was Leadbelly, who had
recently come to New York. His real name was Huddie Ledbetter
and he was an ex-convict, brothel singer, barroom brawler, gam-
bler and two-time murderer. Two years earlier John Lomax, a Li-

brary of Congress musicologist, had discovered him breaking rocks in a Louisiana penitentiary and sponsored his trip north, where he became a legendary folk singer.

The waterfront comrades I knew were themselves prone to burst into song on any suitable occasion and some not so suitable. Their favorites were old Wobbly songs, Irish revolutionary songs, trade union songs. A Filipino seaman wrote "The NMU Love Song" but it wasn't as popular as one that began, "My daddy was a sailor and I'm a sailor, too,/But poor old dad he sailed the seas before the NMU." Another sure-fire winner was made famous by Paul Robeson—"I dreamed I saw Joe Hill last night." Joe Hill, one of labor's long list of martyrs, was a Swedish immigrant who once worked on the docks as a member of the San Pedro longshore local. He joined the IWW and tried to organize the copper miners in Utah, for which the bosses had him executed by dumdum bullets in 1915. He was buried with his longshore union button in his lapel.

Sometimes the singing took place at meetings but mostly it was in bars. One night, after leaving a What's On, a group of seven of us repaired to the Alhambra Bar and Grill in Harlem where, decidedly in our cups, we sang the "Internationale," "Freiheit," and "Bandera Rosa." As we left, the manager said to us, "We certainly enjoyed your college songs."

All the foregoing having been said, it is not meant to denigrate in any way the essential bravery and political awareness of the waterfront members. Their life was by no means all fun and games. Seamen of all countries have traditionally been in the vanguard of the radical movement. For example, André Marty of France, whose father took part in the Paris Commune of 1871, was an ex-boilermaker who in 1919 led the Black Sea naval mutiny. Condemned to twenty years at hard labor, he was released in an amnesty in 1923. In 1936 he organized the International Brigade, composed of 45,000 dedicated men from fifty-two countries, who went to Spain to fight Franco's Fascist rebellion against the democratically elected Spanish government. It was generally supposed that this government was Communist, the usual propaganda lie. In the elected parliament when the civil war began in July 1936, there were only fourteen Communists. The rest was comprised of 98 Socialist Party members, 65 Centrists, 135 Conservatives of the

Right, and 10 Basque nationalists. Franco was financed by Juan March, a Majorcan peasant who couldn't read or write until the age of forty. By smuggling and cheating, he worked his way up to become the owner of a chain of banks and a tobacco merchant. King Alfonso, Spain's last King before the present one, awarded him the tobacco monopoly. During World War I he sold arms to both sides. Later jailed for bribery, he ran his business from his cell, from which he escaped with the aid of a prison guard who retired, rich, to Greece. Juan March's London office was the clearing house for all government trade between Spain and Britain. Naturally, he resented the change from monarchy to republic, especially when he lost his tobacco monopoly.

In 1936 he chartered a plane to fly Franco from the Canary Islands to Morocco. He placed $50 million, plus further credit, at the immediate disposal of the insurgents and continued to finance Franco. He was also active in the deals that brought Mussolini and Hitler into the civil war on Franco's side. One million Spaniards died in the war and two million prisoners were taken by Franco. When his soldiers slaughtered hundreds of women and children in the bull ring of Pamplona, radicals throughout the world gave him the name of The Butcher, but there was not a peep out of the governments of England, France and the United States, who had refused to sell arms to the legitimate Spanish government, although Léon Blum, France's Socialist premier, was ready to send arms for which payment had already been deposited. A telephone call from Stanley Baldwin, the British Prime Minister, persuaded him to cancel the deal. The Rio Tinto mines in Spain, the most important copper mines in western Europe, were British-owned. The proprietors knew they could always do business with the Fascists.

After Franco's victory, Juan March was rewarded with the return of the tobacco monopoly. When he died in 1962 he was the richest man in Spain, worth over $335 million. As for Britain, France and the United States, their leaders kept mum when, to celebrate the victory these same leaders had made possible, Franco let Mussolini's legionnaires march into Madrid first on March 28, 1939. In June there was a special ceremony to honor Hitler's elite Condor Legion which had practiced saturation bombing on April 26, 1937, by destroying the sacred Catholic

Basque city of Guernica. For thirty-seven years Franco maintained his fascist dictatorship with the complicity of the "free world," especially the United States.

More than two thousand American seamen went illegally to Spain to fight Franco. It is possible that some of them were not Communists but the ones I knew were. They realized that if Franco, Hitler and Mussolini won in Spain, the rest of the world would suffer the consequence, which they did in World War II. I had been convinced that this war was coming, ever since Engelbert Dollfuss, the Chancellor of Austria, was assassinated by the Nazis in July, 1934. The Spanish Civil War confirmed my belief and Munich was the clincher. If my Communist friends and I could see that everything pointed to a world war (and this is not hindsight: the Party literature of that time was clear in its warnings and even my own letters foretold what was to come), how is it that the political leaders, the men of power and influence here and in Britain and France, couldn't also read the writing on the wall? Is it possible that they could have been so stupid as to think that the policies of Mussolini, Hitler and Hirohito would not eventually entrap their own countries? I wonder. In 1933, when Hitler first came to power, Winston Churchill, that detestable and immoral man, publicly thanked God "for men like Adolf Hitler." Previously, he had lavishly praised Mussolini and announced that if he had been Italian he would have been "wholeheartedly with him." A. J. P. Taylor, the eminent British historian, has written that Churchill "never intended the overthrow of Mussolini" and "had little sympathy with the idea that World War II was a general crusade against Fascism." Yet Churchill, an egotistical, reactionary, bombastic, blundering, drunken old showoff, always on the side of oppression, with an easily proven record of viciousness, is today a subject for mindless idolatry and, since his death, has been rapidly promoted from "the greatest Englishman" to "the greatest man of the century" to, in one maniacal hyperbole, "the greatest man who ever lived." Forget about Jesus Christ, Buddha, Muhammad et al.

I have gone into this old history because it illustrates the systematic suppression of the truth. A Communist learns to look at history and popular myths with a new eye. Among the first things you learn is that almost everything you've been taught or have

read is either distortion of facts or outright lie. The true documen-
tation is available, but it is not usually publicized in popular
books or the press and other media. Instead, the public is fed
propaganda that nearly always is directed against the Left. William Biddle once wrote in the *Journal of Abnormal and Social
Psychology* that after World War I a favorite instrument of propaganda was to label anyone who disagreed with you a Communist.
He quoted Rob Roy MacGregor, then assistant director of the
power companies of Illinois, as having said, when asked what
method he would use to discredit trade unionists, that he would
spread the word that they were Reds. As a Communist, or Communist sympathizer, I learned to read newspapers and magazines
and books of every political stripe, to compare, to analyze, to
collate the information from all sources. Of any pronouncement I
ask myself: "Who says it? What could be a possible motive?
What else has been said previously by the same person or group?
What people support this pronouncement and what people op-
pose it? Who stands to gain by it and what?" Sometimes the
truth is immediately apparent. Sometimes it doesn't surface for
years.

Communists were active in the formation of the National Maritime Union, just as they were leaders in the struggle against corruption and brutality in the East Coast longshoremen's union.
Communists trying to organize the car industry in the Thirties
were killed or beaten and maimed by Detroit's Black Legion
working for the automobile magnates. Communists were tarred
and feathered in the South, where they were early pioneers for
black equality long before the civil rights movement of later years.
It was the Communist Ben Gold who fought the mobsters Lepke
and Gurrah and drove them out of the Furriers Union. Communists fought corruption, gangsters, Murder, Inc., when the employers used the underworld to crush trade unions. Dutch Schultz
on his death bed cried out, "Mama! The Reds! They're after me!"
And before that, Al Capone had an article published in *Liberty*
magazine (doubtless ghost written but appearing under his
name) in which he attacked Communism.

They were always the first to fight oppression and injustice; and
they were the bravest. When Picasso was asked why he joined the
Party in the Forties, he replied, "Because the Communists are the

bravest in France as they are in my own country Spain." There can be no greater tribute to them than the fact that they are the first targets of Fascism everywhere in the world. The primary aim of Fascism was to smash the trade unions. In order to do this they had to crush the Communists, first in Italy, then in Germany. Mussolini was financed by Giovanni Agnelli, chairman of Fiat and grandfather of the present Gianni Agnelli; by Alberto Pirelli, the tire manufacturing magnate; by Pio and Mario Perrone, owners of the Ansaldo Corporation of Genoa (they first paid him 200,000 lire in 1918); and by other Italian capitalists. These men were not interested in ideologies nor were they Fascist Party members. They simply wanted to protect their profits by keeping wages down. From 1919 to the march on Rome in 1922, Mussolini's strong-arm squads worked for landowners and industrialists as strikebreakers, attacking trade unionists and Socialist demonstrators. The banking association contributed 20 million lire to help Mussolini's coup d'état. He was such a coward he didn't even lead the march on Rome. He waited in Milan, ready to escape to Switzerland if it failed, and then took the night train to Rome when he was sure it was safe. Once in power, he publicly acknowledged Agnelli's contribution to the rise of Fascism and made him a senator. Other industrialists were rewarded with steel and electrical empires.

In Germany industrialists saw Hitler as their Mussolini, and so did he, until he outstripped his model. Fritz Thyssen, chairman of the Ruhr steel trust—he owned iron, coal, steel, electricity and gas works—was the first to see possibilities in the unknown Austrian rabble rouser. After Hitler's abortive Munich beer hall putsch in 1923, he received his first big money from Thyssen, who had called together leaders of industry and banking and advised them to back Hitler. The latter had announced that when he died he wanted carved on his tomb: "Here lies the Final Destroyer of Marxism!" (No wonder Churchill admired him.)

By December 31, 1931, shares in Thyssen's steel trust were quoted on the Berlin bourse at the bankruptcy price of fifteen marks. He needed fresh markets but first he needed to destroy the Communists and Socialists who were the militants of the trade unions. The powerful industrialists Friedrich Flick and Alfred Krupp also became Hitler's early backers along with Hjalmar

Schacht, the financier. Later, Krupp, Flick and the giant chemical firm of I. G. Farben built factories near concentration camps in order to use slave labor. My Communist friends and I knew about these concentration camps even before World War II. How come so many of our democratic leaders profess never to have heard of them until the liberation by Allied troops of Dachau, Auschwitz, Buchenwald and the rest? In 1933 a small group of Communists from the waterfront section went on board the *Bremen* in New York harbor, posing as visitors, handcuffed themselves to the rails and unrolled posters protesting the camps and the persecution of Communists, Jews and trade unionists. They were sent to jail for three months.

We all know that the House of Krupp is now bigger and richer than ever, while when Flick died in 1972 his private fortune was estimated by *The Times* of London as approximately $2½ billion. His industrial empire included three hundred companies, even though when he was convicted of war crimes at the Nuremberg trials, 80 per cent of his companies were confiscated. He rebuilt his fortune after his early release from prison in 1950. He was a personal friend of Konrad Adenauer, who also kept as his right-hand man for fourteen years a Dr. Hans Globke, formerly a Nazi senior official in the Office for Jewish Affairs in Hitler's Ministry of the Interior. And by the way, where was Adenauer during the Hitler years? Not in any concentration camp for opposing the Nazis, that's for sure.

Why rehash all of this? Because it explains why I am a radical, in thought if not in action. Also, because people forget. No matter how often it happens, they never seem to learn the lesson that oppression and tyranny triumph under the guise of fighting Communism, and that the most horrifying brutality of despots is practiced on those they call Communists, whether they are or not. The Greek colonels gained power this way and so did the Chilean junta (with more than a little help from Henry Kissinger, whom Louis Heren of *The Times* of London once described as "the Kissinger of death"). We waged our obscene and criminal Vietnam War in the name of "fighting Communism," and with the same excuse we destroyed the peaceful, neutral country of Cambodia. In Rhodesia, Ian Smith defended the oppression of 400 million blacks by 250,000 whites, announcing blandly that he was saving them from Communism.

It's always this way. The actor Lionel Stander was once quoted as saying, "It's not that I like the Communists so much but that I hate the people who are anti-Communist." Lionel was the first actor to be blacklisted for political reasons, long before McCarthyism swept America. He appeared before the Red-baiting House Committee on Un-American Activities in 1940 and because he did not "co-operate" by naming Communists, he couldn't get another movie job. He was called before the Committee again in 1953, when he defied the inquisitors with such a torrential, nonstop, heroic outburst that Chairman Harold Velde gave up and adjourned the hearing. Lionel told me a few years ago, "I've always been anti-Fascist, anti-Nazi, and I haven't changed. Anyone who isn't interested in politics is an idiot because politics affects your goddamn life. I gave my name and money to any anti-Fascist cause but I never joined any party because I'm a nonconformist. But I never attacked the Communists because the people who did attack them were people I hated."

I feel the same way. I cannot and do not defend the Soviet Union today. I didn't even like Khrushchev, and Brezhnev was no improvement. I am appalled by the suppression of civil rights and personal liberties in Russia, although I also wish that the people who shout the loudest against these abuses would also condemn with equal vehemence the even more terrible regimes with which the United States is on friendly terms and to which we sell arms or even give financial support. An Amnesty International annual report issued at the end of 1975 accused 113 countries of imprisoning people for political beliefs, denying them fair trials, and torturing or killing them. Of 40 governments where the most hideous forms of torture are official policy, Iran and Chile headed the list. Among others nearly as bad were also listed South Africa, Uruguay, Brazil, Argentina and Paraguay, where the government torturers of dictator Alfredo Stroessner (who could not exist without United States aid and support) make Torquemada look like Florence Nightingale. The report added that in India under Mrs. Gandhi there were well over 40,000 political prisoners, while in Indonesia political prisoners were then in their eleventh year of detention without trial, "held under inhuman conditions."

In virtually all the countries where torture and murder of political opponents is official policy, the excuse is the suppression of Communism. I admit that the Communist countries are no paradise and I wouldn't want to live in any of them, with the possible exception of Cuba, but there are Communists everywhere who, usually at great personal danger, are working to make a better world. Therefore, I cannot slobber over the plight of someone like Solzhenitsyn, that multimillionaire "saint." The leaders of a country that lost 20 million dead fighting the Germans cannot be expected to take kindly to a writer who states to the world press that the Nazis were more humane than the Communists and that Russia was better under the czars. Better for whom? I can sympathize with the frustration of writers, artists and such in Communist countries, but revolutions are not made primarily for the benefit of artists and intellectuals. They are made to improve the lot of the masses of workers and peasants, for the victims of colonialism and apartheid. In the Third World today approximately 460 million people live at starvation level, with 300 million unemployed. Even so unlikely a spokesman as Robert McNamara, president of the World Bank, has said that what is needed is "a new world economic order, a change in the world economic structure," although he added, in a British television interview, "Peoples of the West and Japan won't sacrifice to help the poor, but the Third World demand for equality of opportunity among men will force a change."

The Communist parties of England, France, Italy and Spain condemned the Russian invasion of Czechoslovakia. The American Communist Party did not. The European Parties have rejected Moscow's leadership, criticized its policies and pledged support for democratic rights in all countries. They are willing to work with other democratic elements in their respective countries, a move reminiscent of the formation of the Popular Front in 1934. Will it work? I don't know. Previously, a democratic coalition of this type could go just so far, and then came the counterrevolution. The classic example was Spain. As Mao said, "Never in history have the ruling classes voluntarily relinquished power."

Many years ago, at a Socialist convention in Chicago, when someone argued for the gradual acquisition of power through political means, John Reed said: "When the Socialist mayor of Minneapolis wanted to use the police to protect meetings of the workers, his policemen were superseded by a body of special deputies appointed by the governor of the state. When a radical governor of Illinois, Governor Altgeld, tried to use the state power to protect the workers in the Pullman strike in Chicago, President Grover Cleveland sent the U. S. Army into Illinois to protect capital. And if you had a socialist president in the place of Grover Cleveland, the Supreme Court would come to the protection of capital. And if you had a socialist Supreme Court, J. P. Morgan would organize a volunteer White Guard and the interests of capital would still be protected. So it will always be."

The world has changed since those days. (I hope.) Have any lessons really been learned? Looking around me, reading the papers, listening to people talk, I wouldn't think so. How many Americans know, for example what Abraham Lincoln said in his inaugural address on March 4, 1861? He said: "This country, with its institutions, belongs to the people who inhabit it. Whenever they shall grow weary of the existing power, they can exercise their constitutional right of amending it or their revolutionary right to dismember or overthrow it."

Anyone who said those words today would be denounced as a dangerous radical. In Britain the fatuous Mrs. Thatcher and other Tories have been trying to foment a Red scare. It could happen again in America, even though our own Communist Party is small, weak and ineffectual. As for the harum-scarum fragmentation of the New Left, they present a pitiful picture of dozens of small groups more intent on squabbling with each other than uniting in any disciplined, effectively organized approach to Socialism.

I'm glad I'm not young today. I still believe in Marxist theory but I am depressed by too many aspects of its practice. I am even more depressed by the triumph of reactionaries everywhere who continue to gain, or retain, power through the strategy of anti-Communism. It is not very encouraging, and I am often reminded of some lines in a poem by James Russell Lowell which I learned as a child:

> Truth forever on the scaffold,
> Wrong forever on the throne.

Chapter Ten

"SHOW" AND TELL

My husband, Jack Lawrenson, died of Asian flu during the epidemic in the autumn of 1957. In June 1960 I took the children to Europe, paying our way by writing magazine articles to supplement the small amount collected on Jack's life insurance, plus money from the sale of a gypsy moving company, The Padded Wagon, which I ran in Greenwich Village, employing out-of-work actors, indigent artists and writers, and a few former seamen. It was reasonably successful, considering that I had only an old bakery truck which we named Minerva after my mother and, later, another secondhand van called George. However, I was no threat to the Seven Santini Brothers and eventually I realized that I would either have to give up writing and stick to trucking, or vice versa.

The children and I sailed for Naples on an Italian ship, armed with a copy of *Europe on $5 a Day*. Naples, Rome, Venice, Florence. Then Madrid, a wild, wonderful week in Pamplona during the San Fermín festival with the running of the bulls, and Barcelona. Ibiza and Majorca. London, Paris, Geneva. We loved it all so much that in September we said, "Why go home?" I put Kevin in school in Switzerland. Johanna went to Paris, where she lived with three French girls, studied at L'Alliance Française, and became a fashion model. I settled down in the Canary Islands. I lived on $150 a month in a small furnished flat in Las Palmas, with a balcony overlooking the sea, and started trying to write a novel.

In early December I received a telephone call from my agent, Roz Cole, who was in Spain. In the Canaries at that time people had difficulty telephoning each other, never mind long-distance calls. Roz couldn't hear a word I said and the only words of hers I could make out were "Huntington Hartford" and something about a new magazine. I sent her a cable saying, "If job don't want it if article can't he wait." She went home to New York and there followed a comedic exchange of daily cables and letters. On December 13 she cabled, "Hartford will pay economy fare round trip just talk you can return immediately." I cabled back, "How come economy no Canary USA flights anyway." Her December 14 cable said, "Can't you take Lisbon TWA." I cabled her, "Airport here closed storm." (There was no storm.) Her December 15 cable: "Hartford wants you come will cover thousand try arrive soonest." My return cable: "Impossible."

She wrote me that Hartford—she was his agent, too—was going to publish a new magazine which he wanted to make a modern version of the old *Vanity Fair*. When she told him that I had spent four years on *Vanity Fair*, the last twenty-two months as managing editor, he insisted that I come to New York for one day to talk to him. I replied that I was not like Mrs. Eleanor Roosevelt, who at one time was flying all over the world (the State Department code name for her was Rover), and that I simply could not pick up and fly thousands of miles from the Canaries, which are off the west coast of Africa, to Madrid and from there to New York for one day. I said I never wanted to work in another office, but that I would be glad to send Hartford ideas and suggestions gratis.

My recalcitrance apparently only spurred Hunt on. He was accustomed to having people comply when summoned, no matter how remote their whereabouts or at what inconvenience to them. Once, after I was on the magazine, he read in an English newspaper an article by some man none of us, including Hunt, had ever heard of. By means of a deluge of cables and transatlantic calls, he finally tracked the man down to an isolated region of Crete, where the nearest telephone was in a village several miles away. The poor man probably thought he was inaccessible but he didn't know Hunt. The owner of the one village telephone arrived at the writer's cottage by burro with the news that there was an important call from New York and that the writer must call the operator, who would put him through. Naturally curious, the writer obeyed. Hunt talked him into doing a piece for the magazine which arrived eventually. Then Hunt never printed it.

At the time of the Canaries flurry I had not met Hunt but a year or two previously I had talked to him by telephone. I was doing a profile of Errol Flynn for *Esquire*. Flynn had appeared on Broadway as Mr. Rochester in *Jane Eyre*, which Hunt himself had dramatized and produced. I wanted to get some quotes about Flynn from him, so I called and left my name and telephone number. Our phone rang at two o'clock in the morning. I was asleep but my husband, who had insomnia, was reading in the living room and he answered. He came into the bedroom and said, "It's a telephone call for you from Hartford." "Hartford?" I said. "I don't know anyone in Hartford." Then it dawned on me. "Oh! Huntington Hartford!" I picked up the phone. He said that he and his wife had just come home. They were obviously in a festive mood. The conversation was not very productive, interrupted as it was by giggling, whispering, and the sound of merry scuffling on their end. It seemed to me a surprisingly informal call from a complete stranger.

I'm sure Hunt had forgotten about it when he decided to attempt to import me from the Canaries. I thought I had settled that matter and I flew to Paris to spend Christmas with my children. There I received a cable from a friend who lived in my Las Palmas building. She said that Hartford had cabled me $1,000 and she thought I ought to know. I immediately cabled my agent and instructed her to tell Hartford to get his money back, as I had no intention of going to New York. Instead, he had it transferred to a Paris bank, and I received a notice to come and get it. At this point, I gave up. "Kismet," I thought. "At least I can see my mother and my dentist."

I took the plane in January. A few hours out, the pilot announced that New York was closed and we would land in Boston. Some time thereafter, he came on the speaker again to tell us that the entire eastern seaboard was closed and that he was going to try for Newfoundland or, if that wasn't feasible, Greenland. We landed at Gander, where the only available sleeping quarters were occupied by passengers of other planes already stranded there. I sat in the airport all night and sent my agent a wire: "Am in Newfoundland. Wish you and Hartford were here instead."

When I arrived in New York I was exhausted and tense. Roz and I had lunch with Hartford in his Beekman Place duplex, after which I went home to my mother's and threw up. We saw him again for further discussion about the magazine. My first impressions were that he was an attractive man, friendly and courteous, with some intelligent ideas. He was also persuasive. He said he couldn't make me the editor because he had already hired Bob Wool, a young man in his twenties, but that I would have equal power with Wool and complete authority to do whatever I thought necessary to make the magazine a new *Vanity Fair*. His enthusiasm triumphed over my doubts, although I was taken aback when he gave me some paper and told me to write the sentence: "I am walking down the street to get the horse and buggy out of the old garage."

He was a graphology addict and all his employees had to write this sentence. A year or so later, everyone on the magazine had to write it over and over again, without stopping, on yellow, lined, legal pads. All the editors, the art department members, business manager, advertising director and staff—no one was exempt. Hunt called me at home that night to tell me some of the results. He said the handwriting of one of the men showed he had "criminal tendencies." He thought he could judge character and talent from the way a person wrote this one sentence. He was especially interested in g's. Anyone who made a g like a figure eight was supposed to be unusually creative. He must have made an exception in my case, because my handwriting is atrocious.

After I returned to Las Palmas I had second thoughts about the whole deal. I wrote Roz that I didn't think it would work out and that Bob Wool, already hired as top editor, wouldn't be human if he didn't resent me. It would be an impossible situation, I said presciently, and I didn't want any part of it. I was absolutely right, even though I didn't realize the nightmare it would turn out to be. However, I was tired of the Canaries so I went to Tangier, pursued by letters from Roz, saying Hartford was expecting me in April and that everything would be just great. I went back to New York the first of April and met Roz in the coffee shop of the Waldorf. She had my contract with her. After two hours of argument, she overcame my protests—she can sell anyone anything—and I finally signed the contract while sitting on the loo in the Waldorf ladies' room. I should have torn it up and flushed it down.

The *Show* headquarters occupied all of a small, elegant building owned by Hunt on East Fifty-seventh Street. It had once been a mortuary, appropriately enough, as events were to prove. When I showed up for work May 1, Hunt wasn't there and everyone ignored me. I finally got some secretary to direct me to my office, a tiny, bare, inside room with no windows. There was a table and a chair. Nothing else. No typewriter. Not even a pencil. The rest of the staff were in comfortable offices decorated by Melanie Kahn. My office could have been an empty broom closet. When I finally saw Wool he was rude and threatening. When I said good morning to Richard Schickel he turned his back on me. It was hardly an auspicious beginning. Although not excusable, it was understandable. I was the only person on the staff who had been hired directly by Hartford, with the exception of Wool, who had been brought to him by Alan Delynn, a sort of general factotum for Hunt. Wool had hired all the rest. At that time, I was the only one with an established reputation as an editor and writer. The others, including Wool, were trying to make their way up. How could they fail to hate me?

Those first weeks on the magazine were an ordeal I wouldn't wish on anyone. True, some staff members were friendly to me, notably John Erwin, the television editor, and Lou Miano, the theater editor, but Wool, in the first position of authority he had ever held, together with Schickel, his boon companion, ran the whole shebang. Although my contract expressly stated that all material proposed for the magazine should be submitted to me, I was seldom shown anything, nor was I at first allowed to attend editorial meetings. I made lists of suggestions which were ignored. I wasn't even permitted to write anything, with the exception of one caption specifically allotted to me by Hartford. I couldn't keep going to Hunt to tattle. Everything that went in the magazine had to be sent to him for approval and he finally issued an edict that before he saw the material I had to initial it and add my comments. This was done a few times and then forgotten.

The only thing he did insist on was that I should handle his own ideas, of which we had to run two in every issue. The dearest to his heart was what we called the girl feature. I had to interview all the candidates, arrange to have the most promising ones photographed, and write the captions for the ones Hunt chose. They came from all over, wherever they happened to catch Hunt's eye. Every spring he went to Europe and returned with lists of girls. I was kept busy telephoning London, Paris and other cities. Although we were supposed to be a magazine of the arts, many of the girls had nothing whatsoever to do with this area. Once he imported a Finnish girl he had seen working in a Helsinki post office. She came to see me (by then, at Hunt's command, I had been given a secretary and moved to a large, attractive office). She was a lovely blonde who spoke no English but her brother was with her and he could speak a few words. They were both puzzled by the whole bizarre episode, as well they might be. She had no interest in the arts, but I had her photographed, per Hunt's instructions. The pictures were beautiful but Hunt wouldn't use them. He called me to say, "Well, Helen, she wasn't very cooperative. She brought her brother with her."

Hunt's penchant for pretty young girls is legendary. They came into the office by the dozen, and wherever he was, in his various homes in New York, London, Palm Beach, the Bahamas, the South of France, or on his hundred-foot motor yacht, he was surrounded by them. He had them sent in like swatches for his approval. He was often known to leap from a taxi and accost a passing strange girl on the street, giving her his card and asking her to call. Of course they could always say no, and many did.

To enlarge the scope of the search, he made us put a note in the magazine asking for applicants to send in their pictures. In addition, I had to write to a list of girls' schools, requesting nominations; we cased the forty-two girl guides at the United Nations; we scanned fashion magazines, investigated girl winners of music contests, pried into every possible field that might include pretty young girls. Interviewing them, I felt like Florence Reed playing Mother Goddam in *The Shanghai Gesture*. The one featured in the first issue of *Show* was Diane Brown, sent to me by Hunt. She later became his third wife. She was nineteen, a slim, brown-haired, brown-eyed girl with an ingenuous manner. She told me she came from a mining community in Pennsylvania. Trying to establish some connection with the arts proved difficult. She had no ambition for a career in theater or films. "It's too hard work," she said. Did she paint? No. Play a musical instrument or sing? No. She was a model, wasn't she? "No. Not really." Finally, in desperation, I asked, "What *can* you do?" "I can milk a cow," she said, a talent few of us at *Show* could boast.

His other ideas of which I was in charge involved a constant stream of memos to and from Hunt, supplemented by telephone calls from him, frequently to my home at midnight or after, from wherever he happened to be. They were a mixed bag: an article about a British lady poet who wrote *India Love Lyrics* ("Pale hands I loved beside the Shalimar") under the pseudonym of Laurence Hope; a spread of pictures of old cowboy stars (William S. Hart, Bronco Billy Anderson, Buck Jones, Tom Mix, Hoot Gibson, Roy Rogers, etc.); a piece on astrology (Hunt believed that most geniuses are born under the sign of Aquarius); the reprinting of an article written by Caruso about his experience in the great San Francisco earthquake and fire; a monthly page, "What They Are Doing Now," that featured people like Nancy Carroll, Carmel Myers, Serge Lifar, Mae Marsh, Rosa Ponselle, with pictures of them as they were in their heyday, together with photographs especially taken for the magazine.

On the whole, the magazine was impressive to look at, dull to read. Much of the writing lacked polish, style and wit. It may seem incredible, but Hartford's ideas were often the most interesting things in an issue, even though he had to fight to get them in. My attitude to this was that it was his money and his magazine, and that he damn well ought to be able to have what he wanted, especially when it was more entertaining than the rest of the stuff.

The main trouble was that he had no experience as publisher or editor and he was constantly outmaneuvered in the hugger-mugger editorial policies. The history of *Show* would make a McGuffey's Primer of how not to run a magazine. It lost more than $100,000 an issue. In all, Hunt spent an estimated $8 million on it in three years. A lot of this was his fault, although possibly more of it was due to the fact that people who were grinding their own axes took advantage of him.

After seven frustrating months resulting in two disappointing issues, I persuaded Hunt to look for an experienced editor to run *Show* in a top position. It was then that I made a drastic mistake. To get rid of competition, Hunt had bought *Show Business Illustrated*, a flashy Hugh Hefner publication edited by a man named Frank Gibney. I had never met Gibney but we had the same lawyer, Justin Feldman, a good-looking, brilliant man who had been a friend of my husband. With an utterly illogical and ridiculously feminine reaction, every time I thought of Gibney I associated him with Feldman, subconsciously attributing to him the qualities I admired in the lawyer. I kept urging Hartford to see him. Every time Hunt telephoned me to discuss someone else he was considering, I would say, "Have you seen Gibney yet?" I was so persistent that finally he called and said, "I'm going to see your boy Gibney today." He must have liked his *g*'s because he hired him. In the two years that followed, whenever I complained to Hunt, he said, "It's your own fault. You're responsible." A couple of other staff members had warned me earlier, saying, "You don't know anything about Gibney. You've never even seen him."

The moment I laid eyes on Gibney I knew I'd blown it. At his request I met him in the bar of the Carlton Tower. He reminded me of the pictures in the business section of the New York *Times* of men who have been appointed vice-presidents of this or that, and who all look alike. I thought Gibney had that kind of a face. (I wouldn't know him today if I fell over him.) He was puffing on a pipe. I always notice people's hands. His were pudgy and covered with reddish hairs. His manner was cold, severe, authoritarian. "When I am running *Show*," he asserted, "you are never to talk to Hartford, write to him, or communicate with him in any way." I said that practically my only job on the magazine was to execute Hunt's ideas. "I'll decide what you do on the magazine," he said. I learned later that during his first week at work he tried to get Hunt to fire me. Hunt shut him up by saying quietly and firmly, "Frank, I want her on the magazine." Several months later, Hunt remarked in front of my agent, "It's the oddest thing. Every time I mention Helen's name, Frank turns purple."

It wasn't just his treatment of me that made me dislike him.

Arthur Gubernick, our production manager, an acknowledged expert in his field who was responsible for the handsome appearance of the magazine, came to my office in a rage. "Who does he think he is?" he said. Others protested in various ways. I have an inner resilience that protects me, especially from someone for whom I have contempt. The second day Frank was at work, he ordered me into his office to lay down the law. I made some mention of my years on *Vanity Fair*. "I've heard about that and I'm not impressed," he sneered, waving a hand in a gesture of dismissal. I was more amused than angry.

One of his earliest acts was to make us all change offices. There was no imaginable rationale for this, but it accomplished two things. It gave everyone a sense of insecurity and it showed who was Boss. Everyone had to move from his or her office to someone else's, including art director Henry Wolf, who from the beginning had been in a large, light-filled office, the walls of which he had had lined with cork on which to pin photographs and layouts. Even those staff members in small, less desirable offices had grown used to them and were settled in them with their own personal touches of family photographs, desk sets and ashtrays, books and files. We all had to pack up everything and swap places like some idiotic game of musical chairs.

I was assigned to a corner office on an upper floor. It had one window but the space was half the size of the one I occupied. I had a sort of wooden hutch for magazines and reference books. Our original fiction editor, who was on the magazine for only a few months, had designed it and had it built. When she left she bequeathed it to me. I was informed by the moving men that Frank had ordered it not to be taken to my new office. I had it moved there, but only after an unpleasant set-to. As Lou Miano told another editor, "When Helen came out of Frank's office, called him a motherfucker, and slammed his door, I knew there was going to be trouble." A further annoyance was that during the chaotic interchange of offices, no one except Frank was permitted to use the elevator. I had no intention of climbing all the flights to my office, so when I entered the building on moving day I walked into the elevator, pushing past the two very big, very black men in overalls who were guarding it. "You gotta use the stairs, lady," one of them said. "Orders." "Fuck that shit," I said. I figured this approach would work and it did. The man holding the door smiled. He took me up, along with Haskel Frankel, one of our nicer editors. "I'm certainly glad I came in when you did," Haskel said.

When I first started work on *Show* we had eight editors and, of course, Hartford. Counting everyone else except secretaries, there were sixteen on the staff in all, including art department, business and production managers, copy editor and researchers. Almost immediately, Frank raised the number to thirty-four. He also brought with him his general overseer, who frightened the researchers and secretaries. The first time I saw her was in the elevator. "I'm here to crack the whip," she announced, with no preliminaries. "That's nice," I said.

Gibney convinced Hunt that a path paved with gold would lead to success. Glossy color brochures, opinion surveys (proving nothing reliable, as Edsel Ford and Tom Dewey had each once found out), mailing list solicitations, all done by outside organizations, including a publicity agency. "My mailbox is so filled with *Show* sales pitch literature there's no room for regular mail," complained a friend of mine who was already a subscriber.

Then there were the parties. The building had a large room called the gallery. Hunt gave one party there to inaugurate a show of paintings by his ex-wife Majorie Steele and another one that featured an exhibition match by Don Budge and Ellsworth Vines, playing a sort of table tennis Hunt had invented. (The marvelous Pancho Gonzalez was his tennis pro in the Bahamas.) Gibney's parties were on a far more ambitious scale. The first was a large affair in Washington, where I wandered lonely as a cloud until Hunt spotted me and took me with him to introduce me to the more important guests. Among those with whom I shook hands were Lyndon B. Johnson and a textile magnate who tried to make a date with me. After the party, Hunt took a few of us to the Gaslight Club, a Playboy-type establishment. I'm sure I don't know what good any of this did *Show*.

We gave another party at the Plaza in New York and then one at Romanoff's in Hollywood, where I was supposed to be the hostess. Afterward, I wrote Hunt, who was in the Bahamas, "Like all *Show* parties, there were too few top people and too many press agents, freeloaders, secretaries, anonymous girls, and friends of ad agency underlings. No top stars. Only relatives of stars. I think you're wasting a lot of money." Hunt was beginning to complain about the staggering cost. "I'm not a bottomless well," he said to me rather plaintively. Still, it was his fault. He could have put his foot down at any time.

In the office Gibney rewrote everything written by everybody: titles, subtitles, captions, articles. This would have had a demoralizing effect even had he been a better writer. As it was, his obsessive penciling often had dubious results. In a caption of a mere 106 words about Francis Lederer, the actor, he made 26 changes, inserting his own phrases, such as "Lederer, with his Continental smile." What, I wondered, was a Continental smile? He changed "blonde, dimpled Sonja Henie of Norway" to "a Norwegian blonde with dimples named Sonja Henie." When I ventured to point out that this was no improvement, he shouted, "I'm running this magazine and this is the way I want it!"

He sent us a constant stream of memos about style. We were not to use any hyphens; we must stop using "rather," "quite" and "somewhat"; parentheses were forbidden; our sentences were too long; we must cut down on adjectives and also on commas, while the use of semicolons reminded him of "a whooping crane reservation at feeding time." (How's that again?) We must avoid contractions like "can't" for "cannot" or "there'll" for "there will." One memo warned direly that phrases like "producer Smith" or "impresario Zilch" were "irrevocably barred from the pages of this magazine. Any piece of copy that has this locution on it will be automatically killed."

He also conducted pep talks in the library at which attendance was compulsory. Most of us had to sit on the floor. We were not expected to contribute, just to listen. Frank constantly referred to the magazine as "a product." "We've got a product to sell," he would say. "Le's get the product on the rails. Don't fumble the ball." His favorite phrase was "the chain of command." We must all obey the chain of command, he often said.

I tried to quit but I was advised that for the duration of my contract I was forbidden to write for any other publication. Hunt wouldn't release me. I had the children to support and no other source of income. Under duress, I stayed. By the time my contract came up for renewal, I had achieved a modus vivendi and was even writing a few short pieces for the magazine. With Hunt's approval, my new contract stated that nothing in my articles could be changed without my agreement. Frank was furious, but Hunt stood firm.

I was supposed to do four major articles a year. The only ones Frank let me write were Hunt's ideas, which he couldn't veto. I was sent to California to interview a list of film stars but the sole piece I was permitted to do was Hunt's idea of an article about Harry Richman, then a sick old man with dyed hair and Man-Tan, long retired, but with wonderful scrapbooks and memories of his love affair with Clara Bow, the "It" girl, and the days when he sang "The Birth of the Blues" and "Puttin' on the Ritz," and when his club was the talk of New York. I enjoyed doing the piece and Hunt loved it. Frank didn't, but there wasn't anything he could do about it, although he tried. I refused to let him change a word and for once Hunt backed me up. Usually, Hunt would call me and instruct me to see that something he wanted was done on the magazine but not to tell a soul that he had ordered it. This put me in an untenable position.

The Harry Richman piece had an explosive result, through no fault of mine. A man from a promotion agency hired by Frank came into my office and told me that *Show* was going to give a big, elaborate party in New York, bringing Richman as guest of honor and a plane load of other people from California, all expenses paid by the magazine. I thought of course they had cleared it with Hunt, as according to the plans it was going to cost a small fortune. The P.R. man had just left my office when Hunt telephoned me about something else. I said I had been talking about the Richman party. "The what?" he asked. He had been told nothing about it. "Absolutely not!" he said. "Call Frank and tell him it's off. I don't want it and I won't have it." "You call him," I begged. "You know how he hates me." "No, you do it. And this time you can tell him I told you to do it."

Frank wasn't in his office, so I left him a note with the bad news. When he read it, he flew into an apoplectic fit of fury. I had gone to some film preview, but he ordered my secretary, Bernice Daniel, to his office. She was a quiet, intelligent young woman and the best secretary anyone could ever have. "I could tell from his voice the state he was in," she told me later, "and I

began to tremble. I took a Miltown, even though I know they
don't work for twenty minutes." He shouted at her that she was
not to work for me any more but was to be transferred as of that
moment. Then he kept calling me at home until he reached me,
when he launched into a tirade of abuse. He told me never to
come into the office again. I felt like Anna in *Way Down East*
when her cruel father turns her out into the snow with her babe
in her arms, except that the whole episode was silly. I hadn't in-
tentionally let the cat out of the bag. It simply never entered my
head that they would plan such an expensive project without
Hunt's knowledge, especially when it concerned one of his own
ideas.

After that, I stayed home and my salary checks were mailed to
me. Eventually, Hunt got Frank calmed down and he assigned me
to do an article about Joe Culligan, the much heralded wonder
man of advertising who was supposed to save *The Saturday Evening Post*. I worked hard on it, saw Culligan at work, at home,
went to Rochester with him, and interviewed more than thirty
board chairmen, presidents and vice-presidents of the biggest advertising agencies in New York, as well as Dr. Frank Stanton,
then president of CBS, Herb Mayes of *McCall's*, Gardner Cowles
of *Look*, and the big-time financiers involved in the deal. The
piece was a sensation in publishing and advertising circles. It won
me my spurs with Frank. He even wrote me a penciled note,
"Roses are red, violets are blue, Your note was nice and so are
you," decorated with drawings of hearts. I was given an office
again and Frank tried to be friendly. It didn't change my opinion
of him, but I can get along with almost anyone if I try.

Frank sent me to Puerto Vallarta, Mexico, to do a cover story
on the filming of *The Night of the Iguana* and, later, to Mexico
again, with the photographer John Bryson, to do a fifteen-page
feature on the arts in Mexico. To celebrate the publication, another big party was thrown at the Maria Isabel Hotel in Mexico
City, at which I was the hostess. Through my own Mexican con-
nections I had secured advertising contracts for *Show*, including
one with the Mexican Tourist Commission. I came back to *Show*
somewhat of a heroine in Frank's eyes. He offered to send me to
Japan, but I refused. The Japanese connection was one of the
most intriguing things about Frank. From the time he came on
the magazine, there was a stream of Japanese men visiting his

office. Scarcely an issue of *Show* appeared without some mention of Japan: sometimes a review of a Japanese film or book; sometimes a cover by a Japanese artist or an article about some aspect of Japanese life; sometimes a slight item, such as the news that in July 1963 Japan would see an eclipse of the sun. We had two mostly Japanese issues within eleven months. Once I couldn't find a single mention in an issue, until I read Frank's monthly page in the front of the magazine. He was starting a series about the arts in different American cities, a circulation gimmick. This particular one was about Milwaukee, I think. Anyway, Frank's page mentioned something to the effect that in former years when people thought about culture and the arts they thought about London, Tokyo or Paris. Tokyo! He'd managed to slip in the Japanese reference. When he decided to start showing movies in the gallery for invited guests, the first one, to the surprise of no one on the staff, was a long and excruciatingly boring Japanese film with English subtitles. When I left the magazine he was planning articles about Japanese big business—the steel industry in Japan, for one example. You would have thought he was the greatest Japanophile since Lafcadio Hearn.

I couldn't stand it any more, so I ran away, literally. In Mexico I had intimated to Joe Coleman, during a marathon tequila session, that I was fed up. I am a veteran tequila drinker. Joe was not. When I said I didn't want to be associated with it any longer, he argued with me. Did I want more money? I could have it. Was I disgusted by the office atmosphere? I could be Latin American editor, with headquarters in Mexico. "Think it over." I didn't have to think it over. My contract was almost due for renewal again but I left the preceding month without telling anyone.

I sailed for Naples, with Taormina as my ultimate destination. When the ship stopped for a day at Lisbon, I mailed Hunt a letter I had written on board. In it I said that the whole experience had been a harrowing one and that most of the magazine, about which I had no say, despite my position on the masthead, was so boring I couldn't read it, nor did I know anyone who could. "I don't believe even you can read it all the way through," I said. "You threw me to the lions, Hunt."

A few months later Gibney was no longer on the magazine. A friend wrote me that he went to live in Japan as head of the Encyclopaedia Britannica there. "I hope he doesn't rewrite it," I wrote back.

Hunt himself became the editor but later sold the magazine for a pittance to the publishers of *Playbill*. Then he took it back again and made several attempts to revive it. It was a shame, because the idea was valid and with all the money he spent it could have been a great magazine. Instead, the entire venture was a disaster. This, more or less, has been the story of his life. I suppose that in the final analysis the failure of all his projects must be traced back to himself. A shy, emotionally insecure man, he thinks people are always trying to get something out of him, and he is right. When I knew him, he seemed to have no friends or associates who were his peers, either in age or worldly status. He was surrounded by yes-men and sycophants who toadied to him in person and ridiculed him behind his back. On the magazine it infuriated me to see men who lived off him pretending to kowtow to him. They never had the guts to stand up to him, to tell him the truth. They conned him, flattered him, yessed him to death, while among themselves they laughed at him. I resented this. I liked him and, yes, it is true—I felt sorry for him. I fought to defend him.

I think that his immense wealth and the way he has used it made him a target for abuse. Other very rich men hang on to their money and try to make even more. Hunt has spent his life losing money. This is something people cannot understand or forgive.

His father came from Maine to open a small grocery store in New York, which he parlayed into the A&P chain. Hunt's ambition has been to have the press stop always referring to him as "the A&P heir." He has yet to achieve this. Hunt's father, Edward, invented the Hartford shock absorber and made a fortune of his own. Hunt was born April 11, 1911, and brought up in Newport. He never saw much of his father and didn't have anything approaching a normal relationship with him. The father died when Hunt was eleven. His mother, Henrietta, was from South Carolina. With her only son she was domineering and intensely possessive. When Hunt was at St. Paul's boarding school, she rented a house nearby. When he went to Harvard she took a house in Cambridge. In his youth he set off on a voyage in his square-rigger yacht, the *Joseph Conrad*, named after his favorite author. His mother insisted on ordering Walker-Gordon milk delivered to him by plane at every port on his itinerary. Hunt's only sibling, his sister, once was quoted as saying, "Hunt never had a chance."

He inherited from his grandfather and father a fortune at one time estimated at $90 million. He has spent his life trying to get rid of most of it. He has been no useless playboy, flaunting his wealth in giddy jet-set frivolity. Yet because he has unsuccessfully tried to accomplish a variety of projects, he has been jeered and constantly put down. Here are a few of the things he did.

He gave $100,000 to the progressive newspaper *PM* and worked on it as a reporter. (It is always said that he went to work in a Rolls-Royce but he has never owned one.) He went down in coal mines to get stories about miners and he covered Murder, Inc., trials. At that time he was fairly liberal, but he outgrew this, which, if not commendable, is not unusual. He was a competent writer. I looked up an old piece he sold to *Esquire* about his voyage on the *Joseph Conrad*. It was interesting and well written.

He spent nearly $1 million on the Huntington Hartford Theater in Los Angeles, where he produced plays. He also produced and financed a film called *Face to Face* made up of screen versions of two stories. Stephen Crane's *The Bride Came to Yellow Sky* and *The Secret Sharer* by Joseph Conrad. It is still considered by critics a creditable effort. He established and for several years supported an artists' and writers' colony in Pacific Palisades, a suburb of Los Angeles.

He built a Gallery of Modern Art in New York at a cost of about $7½ million and kept it going at an annual operating loss of more than $300,000. His personal art collection cost him $1½ million. He has been criticized and mocked for his taste in art: Constable, John Singer Sargent, Gustave Moreau, Andrew Wyeth, Burne-Jones, Monet, Frederick Remington, Dali, the great Mexican painter Orozco. These are not painters to be sneezed at, and Hunt's dislike of abstract art and the more far-out avant-garde painters is not unique. (As John Lennon once remarked, "Avant garde is French for bullshit.") Personally, I'll string along with Goya. A hundred years from now, or even a thousand, if our planet lasts that long, people who look at Goya's works will understand them and be emotionally moved by them. I cannot imagine they will react the same way to, say, Mondrian,

whose paintings look to me like linoleum designs, or to much of
the modern trash puffed up by publicity into fashionable fads. I
don't go all the way with Hunt, but I go a good stretch.

He spent $2 million on an automatic car parking building, an-
other good idea that failed. He sold it for under $100,000. A
shrewd businessman he is not, although he had a minor success
with a venture he financed to extract oil from shale.

He bought Hog Island in the Bahamas, for $11½ million,
renamed it Paradise Island and spent approximately $15 million
extra to transform the more than seven hundred acres into a
splendid resort. It never really caught on and he sold it for about
a third of his total investment.

He gave a large amount of money to help save the Metropolitan Opera House in New York. For years he tried in vain to
get permission to build a half-million-dollar café in Central Park
for the public. In return for this permission he offered to build a
million dollars' worth of recreation facilities in the Bedford-
Stuyvesant ghetto of Brooklyn. City authorities blocked his café
but he told them they could have the Bedford-Stuyvesant project
anyway.

And, of course, there was *Show*, originally intended as a beautiful and sophisticated magazine devoted to the arts.

These were not bad things he tried to do with his money. They
were unsuccessful but at least he kept on trying. He has not been
afraid to fail. He is a stubborn, willful idealist. Yes, he is interested in astrology, but the public would be amazed at the number
of men and women throughout the world who refuse to make a
move without consulting their astrologists. Hunt never went that
far into it and anyway I don't care if he ran his life by consulting
the entrails of a goat. As for the handwriting bit, the army has
used graphologists to help determine character and so have criminal courts in several countries. I may not believe in it and you
may not, but that doesn't prove it has no value.

I don't know why I should go to the trouble of championing
him when he was basically responsible for my nerve-racking time
on *Show*, except that I am tired of the Huntington Hartford myth.
I honestly wish that just once he could succeed in one of his
projects and be given the credit for it.

Chapter Eleven

───◆───

AND CLARK GABLE SAID TO ME

I have been interviewing celebrities for more than fifty years. I have a reputation as one of the best in the field. In an article about me that appeared a few years ago in *Viva*, Rosemary Kent said that for many years I have been "the writers' writer, whose articles are cherished, even pored over like school primers, by both aspiring and established writers."

It would be difficult to find many people with a personality less suited to the profession. I am not gregarious; I dislike meeting strangers; I hate the role of interrogator. I refuse to ask impertinent questions about people's private lives and if they themselves bring up something intimate, as they sometimes do, I am so embarrassed that I change the subject. I am easily deterred. Unlike Oriana Fallaci, the celebrated Italian woman journalist, I don't keep after people or besiege them. I'll take no for an answer. It's never that important to me. Actually, few people have refused me an interview, although I'm relieved when they do. One of them was Orson Welles. He was supposed to have said, "Under no circumstances would I ever permit myself to be interviewed by Helen Lawrenson." If correctly reported, he was in error, as at the time I admired him and considered him one of the authentic geniuses of the cinema.

Contrary to the opinion of some, I do not do hatchet jobs. There are a lot of things I will not do for money. One of them is to betray my political principles and another is deliberately to write an inaccurate profile. I never go to an interview with a preconceived "angle." I let the story evolve from the interviews. I try to be fair. Some women journalists seem obsessed with their own importance and demand to be treated like queens. I've occasionally been treated like a doorstep salesman but I would never dream of writing an unkind piece just for the sake of retaliation. Furthermore, if anyone asks me not to mention something, I don't mention it.

I have liked many of the people about whom I have written but I never become friends with them the way photographers and other journalists often do, including the French girl reporter who interviewed Gregory Peck and married him. I interviewed Peck in Red Rock Canyon in the Mojave Desert when he was starring in *The Big Country*. A company of 240 was transported into the Mojave at a location cost of $35,000 a day. We all had to be up by 5:30 in the morning and if I never see a desert again it will be much too soon. I thought Peck was handsome, courteous and more intelligent than I had expected, although I can't hand him much as an actor. Anyway, I never saw him again. Once an interview is over, I avoid even those persons I really liked and with whom I got along well. If I should see one of them on the street I would duck into a doorway.

Another thing is that I get bored with an interview long before they do. If I force myself, I can come on strong but I can't sustain the effort. There comes a moment when I think, "Oh, fuck it. How can I get away?" I never stay as long as I'm expected to. I was supposed to spend a week in Berlin for a profile of Michael Caine, but I left after three days, although I think that I probably liked him the best of anyone I've ever interviewed. He's exceptionally intelligent, well informed, perceptive, witty, kind, thoughtful, with no side, not a smidgen of anything phony. He's also a fine actor. But I just can't stand hanging around movie sets. It's boring and exhausting.

In fact, I can't stand long interviews, not just with actors but with anyone. I was the first journalist Yves Saint Laurent ever invited to his home, which he did after I had previously met him in his office. We had an excellent lunch and I liked him. He's a bright man and a nice person. We were getting along great, but I believe in quitting when I'm ahead, so I looked at my watch and muttered something about having to leave. *"Mais je suis désolé!"* Yves exclaimed. (We spoke only French as at that time his English was practically nonexistent.) "I thought of course you would spend the afternoon." I made up an excuse about another engagement.

I did the same thing with Jeanne Moreau when I had lunch with her in her Paris flat. She is a superb actress who has become internationally famous for her portrayals of women racked by passion. One has only to see on the screen her moody, melancholy face with its tired and troubling beauty, that small, full, sullen mouth—and you feel that here is a woman who knows what sex is all about. Every moment she is on the screen she projects sensuality. She does not look young or cute or innocent or helpless. She looks susceptible and smoldering.

Off screen she seems younger and healthier. She has pretty little hands ("Japanese hands," Marcello Mastroianni called them) and she gestures with them as she talks in a quick, light voice, slipping into French occasionally, but mostly in English. (Her mother was English, a member of the Tiller Girls troupe who went from London to Paris to dance in the Folies Bergères.) She was the perfect hostess, pouring my champagne, lighting my cigarettes, solicitous about the food. She made one rather odd remark. We were discussing how many older men trade in wives their own age for younger women, after twenty-four years or so of marriage. Like Nelson Rockefeller did, and Henry Ford, for example. Moreau said how unfair it is, and I said that it is simply one of the facts of life that women have to face. Then she said to me, "You're lucky your husband is dead. At least you know where he is." That was not precisely the way I felt about it, but I suppose she was just being realistic. Otherwise, she was gracious, demure, polite—and guarded, with a nice display of that neat, deft, spiky, impermeable French charm that's like going smack into a wall of frozen treacle. I had to escape. She is one of the few actresses whom I will go to see, no matter what the film, and I was fascinated by meeting her, but I left so unexpectedly that I'm sure she thought me rude. She certainly acted surprised at my abrupt departure.

I think the reason I seldom stay the course is because in meeting these strangers I have to establish, however temporary, a rapport. I have to try to break through their professional veneer to the human being. This takes effort, skill, intuition, diplomacy. I have to put out in order to extract from them. I have learned how to do it, but it is tiring. Even now, after all these years, when I am on my way to a first interview, I often think, "I cannot do it. I'll run away. I'll disappear."

This may stem partly from my reluctance to go through the inanity of average preliminary small talk. The weather, the view from window or terrace, the autumn foliage or spring flowers, the traffic problem. In my family it is known as my "How were the roads?" routine, because many years ago, stuck with someone's uncle and aunt who had just driven from Michigan to New York, I could think of absolutely nothing to say to them or they to me. Finally, I incredulously heard myself asking, "How were the roads?" They proceeded to tell me at some length, as if I gave a damn. Ever since, at parties—which I avoid if possible—I sometimes, after a few drinks, repeat the question to innocent strangers, leaving them utterly nonplussed.

Some people are easier for me than others. When I interviewed Mike Nichols for a *McCall's* article about "Manhattan's Most Fascinating Men" (their idea; certainly not mine), we met for lunch at Sardi's. The first thing he said was, "This is so embarrassing. I don't know why I do it." I told him he wasn't any more embarrassed than I was and that I always feel like a fool, sitting with some stranger, asking him what his hobbies are. Nichols is possibly the brightest man I've ever interviewed. He has a mind like a laser beam, and his wit is not dependent on wisecracks. Instead, it is a deadpan mockery of the banal, the swift impalement of a cliché. The *McCall's* editors had insisted on giving me a list of supposedly helpful "guidelines" for my interviews with the men they had chosen for the article. Notice if their shoes are shined. (Was I supposed to peer under the table?) What do they think is the most important thing in a woman? Do they dance?

Mike and I had a lot of fun with these and we also had a lot of drinks and forgot to eat. The result was that I was late for my next appointment, which was with Emmett John Hughes, then the eminent political pundit for *Newsweek*. He had allotted me fifteen minutes only, because he was expecting Hubert Humphrey, at that time the Vice-President. Late, breathless and tipsy, I rushed into his office, said, "Do you dance?" and burst out laughing. I imagine he must have thought, "Who is this idiot woman *McCall's* has sent to interview me?"

There is never any problem with David Niven because he does most of the talking. He's completely at ease and immensely entertaining. I met him first in the bar of the Connaught Hotel in London and later flew to the South of France to lunch with him and his stunning wife, Hjördis, at their house overlooking the sea at Cap Ferrat. His first autobiographical book, *The Moon Is a Balloon*, had not yet been published and he had no idea it would turn out to be a tremendous best seller. He has a vast fund of consistently amusing anecdotes and I enjoyed listening to him, except that, as usual, I left precipitately, even though it meant that I had to sit for three hours in the Nice airport waiting for my London plane. The one hitch was that before *Esquire* could publish my article, the book came out and Niven was on every TV and radio show, telling exactly the same stories he had told me. My piece would have been just repetition, so *Esquire* killed it.

It embarrasses me when this happens, because I dislike taking up someone's time for interviews and then nothing appears in print. It doesn't seem to bother some writers, but it does me. Fortunately, it seldom happens. It did with Rock Hudson, though. I went to California to do several articles for Clay Felker's *New York* when it was still a section of the Sunday *World-Telegram-Herald-Tribune*, or whatever that amalgamation was called. Then the whole paper folded before I got around to writing the pieces. The public relations man, Rupert Allan, had taken me to Rock's house for lunch. I didn't expect to like him, but I did. He turned out to be a modest, unaffected, rather shy man, with no discernible vanity about his stardom or his good looks. At 6′4″ he towers above a lot of male stars who, like Sinatra or Richard Burton, for example, sometimes have to stand almost on tippy-toe to match their female leads. He has no high-faluting notions, either, about his acting. He said that when he was a kid, Roy Harold Scherer, Jr., in Winnetka, Illinois, he wanted to act and tried out for school plays but never got a part because he couldn't remember his lines. His father was an auto mechanic, his mother a telephone operator. Rock started working after school when he was ten. Before he became an actor he had worked as a mailman, golf caddy, window washer, short-order cook, soda jerk, piano mover and truck driver. He first went to California with the idea of attending UCLA but failed his exams. "I used to stand in front of movie studios, hoping to be 'discovered,' but no one ever noticed me." A fellow truck driver had a friend who had a friend who knew an agent. "He got me a screen test and it was so poor that for years they showed it to beginners' classes as an example of bad acting. When I finally landed a bit part, I muffed my lines thirty-eight times."

Nevertheless, he became a star. For a whole decade he made the Ten Top Boxoffice Stars list every year and for four years he was named World Favorite Film Actor by the Hollywood Foreign Correspondents Association. In one year alone he received fourteen national and international awards and in 1957 he was nominated for an Oscar for his part in *Giant* opposite Elizabeth Taylor, although he didn't win. Actually, what he wanted to do, he told me, was to appear in a musical. Last year he made it, playing King Arthur on tour in *Camelot*. He is crazy about opera and other classical music and is great friends with the singers Beverly Sills and Marilyn Horne. In fact, everyone seems to like him, possibly because he never says an unkind word about anyone. The nearest he came to it was when I asked him if Jackie Onassis, then Jackie Kennedy, was as attractive in person as in her photographs. He hesitated. Then he said, almost reluctantly, "Well, let's just say that she's photogenic."

Sometimes I see people for only an hour or two and it's enough. Meeting them face to face, I can get the vibrations, winkle out a clue to what they're like beneath the glossy surface. Others I have to see several times—at work, at home, at play. I know there are writers who can spend weeks bird-dogging their subjects. Not me. When I first met Laurence Harvey for lunch, he ebulliently suggested that I come and stay with him in his London flat for a week, the better to observe him. I recoiled in panic. We compromised with a session at home with him and another at a film studio. I think he was a better actor than most people gave him credit for being. I'll never forget his performance in *Room at the Top*, with Simone Signoret, which I have seen half a dozen times.

Signoret, by the way, is one of the few women actresses with whom I got along well and whom I really liked. (The others were Lilli Palmer, Deborah Kerr and Juliette Greco.) She has a straightforward frankness and a warmth that are quite un-French. She is obviously all woman. When we were talking about sex one day during lunch, she said to me, "When I am an old lady of seventy-five, people will look at me and think, 'She really *liked* it!'"

She also has one of the sexiest husbands around, Yves Montand. He took me to lunch at the Four Seasons in New York and I was completely flummoxed by his charm. I was surprised to learn that he doesn't have a drop of French blood. He was born Ivo Livi in Tuscany, the son of a poor Italian peasant who was a political militant against Mussolini and fled with his family to Marseille, where he worked on the docks. Yves himself went to work at the age of eleven and was variously a factory worker, waiter, bartender and hairdresser. At eighteen, he began his theatrical career as a dancer in a Marseille theater and eventually went to Paris, where he became the friend and protégé of Edith Piaf, who started him on his singing career, before he took up acting. He's one of the best film actors I've ever seen and, like Moreau, one of those very few whom I will go to see in anything. Even in bad films he's good, while in ones like *Wages of Fear, La Guerre East Fini,* and Z, he is marvelous.

I met Deborah Kerr in Puerto Vallarta, Mexico, where she was filming *The Night of the Iguana* with Richard Burton and Ava Gardner. It was a hectic week. Burton was drinking Mexican boilermakers—straight tequila with beer chasers. He and Elizabeth were not yet married but she was there with him, looking blazingly beautiful. No one introduced me to her and I am incapable of going up to someone like that and introducing myself, although years later I met her in Paris, where all she said was "How do you do?" and all I said was "Hello." What on earth do you say to Elizabeth Taylor? As for Ava, she was her usual self with the press, aimiable as an adder. I had met her some years before, at which time, when told that I was a journalist, she looked as if she had suddenly come face to face with the Abominable Snowman.

The nicest, sanest person in the whole kit and caboodle at Puerto Vallarta was Deborah. She and her husband, Peter Viertel, lived apart from the others in a house on the opposite side of town, away from all the tempestuous brouhaha that raged elsewhere. I went over there twice and found it a refreshing oasis of calm. "It would serve them all right," Deborah said, "if I suddenly developed temperament, had hysterics, became an unmanageable sexpot, threw temper tantrums or something, but I suppose I won't. I'll do my job the best I can, and Peter and I will try to live as normal a life as possible under the circumstances."

What I didn't tell her was that she was the unwitting cause of a humiliating incident in my life. I saw *The Journey*, costarring her and Yul Brynner, three times and was so impressed by her poise, her air of well-bred distinction, that I decided to try to speak in a low voice, buy my clothes at Abercrombie & Fitch and act like an upper-class English lady. I bought an expensive black wool skirt, a gray cashmere cardigan, although I look ghastly in gray, and a single strand of cultured pearls. I usually wore a tailored white silk shirt under the sweater but one day in Paris, when I was doing an article about Chanel, I went to talk about her with the editor of Paris *Match*. It was a warm day and I didn't put on the blouse. Sitting in the editor's office, with him behind a massive desk, we carried on our conversation in French. Absent-mindedly, I unbuttoned the cardigan and drew it open. The editor never batted an eyelash but continued speaking, his face impassive. We finished talking, I thanked him politely and left. The young French woman who had brought me there was waiting outside. She took one look at me and exclaimed, "*Mon Dieu!*" It was only then that I looked down and realized that I had been sitting in the editor's office like some demented middle-aged stripteaser. Heaven only knows what he thought of my performance.

The week in Puerto Vallarta was the longest stretch I've done on any one article, with the exception of about ten days in Spain with Anthony Quinn. He was living with Yolanda Addolori, to whom he was not then married, and their two small sons, in a luxurious rented house, complete with swimming pool. I saw him there, day after day; and I also flew with him and his male employee to San Sebastian, where we rented a car and drove to Pamplona and other Basque towns. Whoever lives with Quinn lives in turmoil. I learned to accept this, along with his volatile temper and restless moodiness. He projects an aura of explosive maleness, a taurine sex appeal that magnetizes women, a quality of which he is not exactly unaware. I admired him, respected him and got along with him, except that it was more physically demanding than my usual interview experiences, especially when I had to climb a mountain. There was no reason for the climb. It was not part of the film. Quinn just wanted to do it, and he insisted that I come along, although he told me to take a less difficult path than the one he chose. I am among the least athletic of persons and have always subscribed to a statement attributed to Robert Hutchins when he was president of the University of Chicago. He is supposed to have said, "Whenever I feel the urge to exercise I lie down until it passes."

Quinn went off in high spirits, saying he would meet me at the top. Together with two press agents I laboriously huffed and puffed my way up the mountain, a feat not made any easier by the fact that I was wearing opera pumps with what used to be called Cuban heels. I didn't have any other shoes with me, not having envisioned any sporting endurance test. Once at the top, we sat down and waited. No Quinn. After about an hour we decided to go back down to the film location. This presented a more difficult problem than the ascent. I suffer from vertigo and can never sit in a theater balcony or look out anyone's office window or from a penthouse terrace. The P.R. men suggested that I ride down on a burro, but the burro looked even more decrepit than I felt. We finally went slowly down, one P.R. man in front of me, with my hands on his shoulders, and the other behind me, with his hands on my shoulders. I didn't dare look and kept my eyes closed part of the time. We eventually made it. The director and crew were sitting around, waiting for Quinn. When he hadn't appeared after two hours, I suggested that someone ought to go and look for him. "Oh no," I was told. "He often goes off by himself to think."

It was some time later before he showed up. What had happened was that he had fallen into a deep crevasse. He kept trying to climb out but slipped back every time. He believed that of course they would send a search party. Finally, he thought, "Christ! Nobody's going to come." By sheer guts he managed to pull himself up, emerging with bruised hands and legs. There was no filming that day. Quinn went home to recuperate. I went back to my hotel and to bed. There must be an easier way to earn a living, I thought.

I met my first movie star when I was five. She wasn't in movies then, though. She was called "Cuddles" and she was one of a group of children managed by Gus Edwards, who taught them to sing, dance and recite, and booked them on vaudeville tours. The troupe came to Syracuse and Cuddles stayed at our house, together with a boy named Georgie Price, who became a well-known comedian and then a rich stockbroker. The reason they stayed with us was because J. Walter Rubin, then a Syracuse lawyer, later a top executive of one of the largest film companies, was a friend of my father and also of the local vaudeville theater manager. I suppose it was cheaper to park the children with friends than at a hotel, and also they would be looked after and kept out of harm. Anyway, Cuddles grew up to become Lila Lee, a Hollywood star of silent films, who played opposite Rudolph Valentino. Although I felt I had a personal interest in her, I could never forget that as Cuddles she wore her long hair parted in the middle, with two braids coiled and pinned like doughnuts on each side. My mother was intrigued by this and made me wear my hair that way for several years. I hated it. Grownups thought I looked "cute," but other children made fun of me.

I started interviewing when I was nineteen, just out of Vassar and working on a Syracuse newspaper. Most of my subjects were visiting lecturers like Clarence Darrow, musicians like Fritz Kreisler, Mischa Elman, Jascha Heifetz, writers like Edna St. Vincent Millay and John Cowper Powys, politicians (Franklin D. Roosevelt when he was governor of New York, and Al Smith); golf champions, prize fighters, Lindbergh, Admiral Richard Byrd, the explorer, and important business tycoons. The president of the Waterman pen company, Mr. Waterman himself, gave me a fountain pen, the only gift I've ever received from anyone about whom I've written, with the exception of one from Sally Rand, the fan dancer. She sent me a white satin evening bag, fitted with powder compact and lipstick, after I put her picture in *Vanity Fair* magazine. Oh yes, and Fleur Cowles, about whom I wrote for a small magazine called *Park East*. A man with a brief case rang the bell of my Greenwich Village flat. I was about to say, "We don't want any," when he announced that he was from Cartier's. Mrs. Cowles had sent me a gold ring which she herself designed. I was embarrassed but not enough embarrassed to send it back.

With the exception of the incomparable Al Jolson, most of the theatrical people I interviewed during my newspaper days were former silent-screen stars making vaudeville tours, among them Betty Blythe, a statuesque brunette siren, and Anita Stewart, whom I had seen every week in a serial called *The Goddess*, when I was seven. Accompanying her on her vaudeville tour, although not appearing himself, was her young husband, a Peabody of the Boston Peabodys. I imagined that when he was a little boy she was his favorite movie star, so he grew up and married her.

After I went to work on *Vanity Fair* in New York, I naturally met a great many stage and film stars of the Thirties, mostly at Condé Nast's parties or other social gatherings, so I didn't have to endure the ordeal of interviewing them, although I could never quite get used to dining at Condé's with Bebe Daniels, drinking at the Atlantic Beach Club on Long Island with Richard Barthelmess, Harold Lloyd and Phyllis Haver, or chatting at parties with Gloria Swanson, all of whom I had seen in films when I was a child. I was especially impressed by Gloria, who had the most fabulous eyes I've ever seen, dazzling blue-green, like magnificent jewels. I figured she was only about ten years older than I was, if one accepted the premise that she went into movies at fourteen. She was a movie extra in 1913. Twelve years later, she was the Marquise de la Falaise de Coudraye, having already married and divorced Wallace Beery and Herbert Somborn; and she was known around the world as Gorgeous Gloria. Temperamental and galvanic, she really made things hum, a Movie Queen in the grand manner. She wore clothes dripping with ermine tails, monkey fur, sequins, seed pearls, marabou, ostrich feathers; and her Hollywood house was famous for its black marble bathroom with gold-plated tub. She lived extravagantly, cosseted by butlers, maids and four secretaries. By the time I met her socially, she had had another husband and was a frequent companion of Joe Kennedy, the Kennedy clan patriarch, who bought RKO Pictures for her so that she could make a comeback in talkies.

The celebrities I met professionally as a magazine editor were not difficult because I wasn't doing what came to be called "indepth" profiles. I seldom had to talk to them for more than a few minutes when I had them photographed for *Vanity Fair*, as we ran their pictures with captions, not articles. I remember George Raft because when he came into the office I was surprised at how short he was, despite his built-up shoes. He was wearing a long white muffler that fell to his knees. "That's quite a scarf, Mr. Raft," I commented. "It's real silk," he said. "Go ahead—give it a feel." He kept assuring me that he was a "perfect gentleman" who neither smoked nor drank. I knew that he came from Hell's Kitchen, one of eleven children in a German-Italian family, and that he owned a photograph of the gangster Owney Madden inscribed, "To Gigolo Raft, the black snake from 10th Avenue." He looked aghast when I mentioned this. At the time, he was up for the role of Popeye in the film version of Faulkner's *Sanctuary*. He hadn't read the book. "What kind of a guy is this Popeye?" he asked me. I tried to explain but he cut me short. "Oh, I get it. Sort of a Dr. Jekyll and Mr. Hyde." I gave up. (Jack LaRue got the part, possibly because Raft thought it would be bad for his image.) Lusha Nelson, our staff photographer, took a terrific picture of Raft looking appropriately sinister, and I wrote an ornate caption: "In the icy menace of his eyes, the motionless deadly tension of his face, there emanated some dark and beautifully reptilian quality which caught the public imagination like a flame." Wow.

In later years my children were never awed by my contacts with the famous. They responded with apathy whenever I took them to the movies and would say of Fredric March, Charles Boyer, Bette Davis, Peter Lorre, Maurice Chevalier and so on, "I had lunch with him" or "I met her when I had her photographed for *Vanity Fair*." They took it for granted that I probably had met everyone. After listening to a radio play about Lillian Russell, my daughter Johanna, then ten, called out, "Mommy, did you know Lillian Russell?" "Darling, she was in the nineteenth century!" "Well, did you know her?"

Their favorite stars were different from mine. When I went to Hollywood to visit Joan Crawford, all my four-year-old son Kevin was interested in was an autographed picture of Fess Parker. He was an avid fan of Parker's adventures as Davy Crockett. He had a Davy Crockett raccoon hat with bushy tail and, brought up among the roistering merchant seamen who were our friends, used to sing the Crockett song lines "Killed him a bear when he was only three" as "Killed in a bar when he was only three." Johanna's favorite was Betty Hutton, whom she saw in films and whose strident-voiced records she played nonstop while doing her school homework. And, of course, they both followed the Lone Ranger radio series and used to chant gleefully: "Hi-oh, Silver, everywhere, Tonto lost his underwear. Tonto say, 'Me no care, Lone Ranger buy me 'nother pair.'"

They had never heard of Marlene Dietrich. One day in the summer of 1951 our telephone rang and Johanna answered it. "It's some lady named Marlene something," she said. I was supposed to interview Dietrich for *Esquire* and had gone about it in the customary way by contacting the press agent for her forthcoming film. He was supposed to set it up but apparently he decided to let Dietrich and me work it out, so he gave her my telephone number. After that first unexpected call, when she said she couldn't make it that week but would be in touch, she called every four or five days, until it got so that whenever the phone rang Kevin would shrug his shoulders and say, "Probably Marlene Dietrich again." The calls went on for three weeks. She made dates and broke them, all in that low, mysterious voice. Once, her husband called. "This is Rudolph Sieber," he said and added quickly, "I am Marlene Dietrich's husband." I had sent her a wire, suggesting that we stop playing ring-around-the-rosy and get it over with. Mr. Sieber said he had read the telegram and then called his wife, who was in the country. She asked him to telephone me and make a definite appointment. In due course, she herself telephoned and broke it. Her excuse was always the same: She had to take care of her grandsons. She was apologetic and charming. Obviously, if she hadn't been willing to see me, she wouldn't have telephoned in the first place. I found out later that at the time she never did anything without consulting her astrologer. Apparently he (or she) finally decided that the propitious time had arrived. Dietrich telephoned at 1:30 in the afternoon. I was in blue jeans and a man's work shirt, with my hair in pigtails, doing the family washing. "Could you meet me in half an hour in the ladies' bar of the St. Regis?" she asked. I gasped. "I am so sorry it is such short notice," she went on. "If it is not convenient for you, please, we will make it another time." I told her I could make it within an hour. I flew around like some mad Keystone Kop comedy and managed to get there only a half hour late. She was waiting for me at a small table, sipping lemonade. She wore a plain gray dress, a black velvet beret on her yellow hair, and no jewelry. Light lipstick and a touch of powder were the only make-up on that pale, magic face. ("Those cheekbones! I could photograph that face for the rest of my life," one photographer said.)

She wasn't in the least annoyed by my lateness. Her voice was low and slow, her manner quiet, her expression serene and

amused, as if she had seen the rise and fall of empires and knew
the score exactly. Somehow, this immeasurable inner poise, this
tranquillity, was part of the secret of her allure. She never fidgets.
Not once while I was with her did she fuss with her hair, look in
her mirror, wave her hands or raise her voice. She sat there
quietly, relaxed and lovely. When she had nothing to say, she
kept silent. "I am not mysterious or enigmatic," she explained. "I
am truthful. When you do not chatter, when you do not make
superficial small talk, people always think there is something
strange about you."

I knew what she meant, but I guess you have to look like that
to get away with it. George Wiswell, a friend of mine on *Esquire*,
had met her at a cocktail party some months earlier. "I was talking to Jinx Falkenberg," he told me, "and thinking how great-
looking she is, when someone brought Dietrich over. Effortlessly,
she stole the show. Jinx wore a perfume I had thought very nice,
but Dietrich had a perfume that made the other one disappear."

She had that effect on men, and on women, too. Ernest Hemingway said of her, "She's the best that ever came into the ring."
Not in movies, though. In her pre-Hollywood German film *The
Blue Angel*, she was a rather chubby, but sexy, low-class music
hall entertainer. Then Hollywood brought her to America and
transformed her into a beautiful zombie: blank stare, immobile
face, expressionless whisper. The face was spellbinding but the
acting was terrible. As one Thirties critic said of a Dietrich film,
"She never looked more beautiful—or more dumb."

America has produced one truly great film actor, Marlon
Brando, and some very good ones like Rod Steiger and George
Scott. I've never met Scott but I talked to Steiger several times
during the making of *Doctor Zhivago* in Spain. He's not only an
actor of integrity and depth but an extremely intelligent and artic-
ulate conversationalist. He can talk well on any subject and you
forget that he is an actor, which is more than I can say for many
members of the profession who are always self-consciously "on"
when confronted by anyone from press, television or radio. The
older generation of English actors are the worst in this respect,
trapped in the tradition of the quintessential British-officer-and-
gentleman (which Leslie Howard, really a Hungarian named
Steiner, did better than any of them), the paragon of pseudo-
modesty and reticence, who would prefer death by lapidation to

the use of the first-person pronoun. When I asked Trevor Howard if he still plays cricket, he replied, "One does occasionally. Of course, one isn't as good as one used to be."

As for Brando, I interviewed him when he was twenty-seven. He made a haunting impression on me. I had only seen him on the stage as the muscular, bellowing Stanley Kowalski of *A Streetcar Named Desire*. He already had a Hollywood reputation as a recalcitrant nonconformist, so I was prepared for the worst. The editors of *Mademoiselle* arranged for me to lunch with Brando and Yul Brynner and to be photographed with them afterward. On the appointed day, Brynner arrived at the magazine office on the dot. We sat there and waited for Brando. After nearly an hour we called his apartment. He had forgotten all about it and was still asleep. Shortly thereafter, he appeared, looking tousled and uncomfortable. During the introductions he stared at his shoes, scowling. No word, no smile, no nod. I wouldn't have been surprised if he had turned his back and walked out. In contrast, Brynner was all charm and sophistication. He was well groomed and wore an expensive-looking gray suit, gray shirt, gray silk tie. Brando had on a rumpled brown suit, a checked sport shirt and an old pullover green sweater. When we got in the elevator it was crowded with girls going out to lunch. They took one gander at my two escorts and conversation stopped dead. The intensity of their stares all but burned up the oxygen. Brando looked as if he wished he had stayed in bed.

The restaurant was called the Hapsburg. It was one of those places with a handwritten menu a yard long, everything in French. Brando studied it and then said he wasn't hungry. "I'll take a peanut butter sandwich," he said. The headwaiter, hovering solicitously, reacted as if about to keel over in a faint. Brynner saved our honor by ordering wine with the air of a man of the world who knows what's what. He also ordered a sirloin steak, rare. Brando suddenly developed an appetite. "I'll take one of those, too." He had brought with him a copy of Stendhal's *Le Rouge et Le Noir* and he opened it. For a desperate moment, I thought he was going to read throughout the meal, but he and Yul started talking about chess, which I don't play. Parcheesi is more my speed. Eventually, I cajoled them into answering a few questions. I got Brando's name wrong twice, calling him Marlo Brandon. "Just call me Leonard," he said. I realized he was trying to be friendly but wasn't quite sure how. He slouched over the table, shuffled his feet, twisted in his chair, played with the silverware. Physically, there was an unquiet beauty about him, with a far more poetic face than shows on screen. His hair then was chestnut and disheveled, his skin had a creamy pallor. His eyes are a dark and disturbing blue-gray. "Someone once said they're the color of seagulls' shit," he said. "It's good fertilizer but not as good as bats'."

He was obviously ill at ease. He told me that he wasn't sure he wanted to be an actor. He thought maybe he wanted to be a writer and said that he kept working at it but would never show it to anyone. "I still don't know what I want to do with my life." Moody, thoughtful, driven by some inner demon of unrest, he seemed to me a poignant young man. I believe that his reputation for rudeness and hostility stemmed from his unwillingness to compromise with phoniness and his deep distrust of the glitteringly glib arena in which he found himself. It was not a pretense. Looking at him, I thought of Thomas Wolfe's *Look Homeward, Angel* and the lines, *"Which of us has known his brother. . . . Which of us is not forever a stranger and alone?"* On the street, when we left the photographer's studio, Brando put his arm around me and said, "I don't mean to be unco-operative. You must forgive me. It's just that I'm no good at this sort of crap."

There have been times when I have said that I would never interview another film star. It has been a relief to get away from them and to see, instead, such divers types as Onassis, J. Paul Getty, André Previn, Nabokov, an Italian princess, the Duke of Bedford or Danny McGarvey, head of the British Boilermakers Union. Always, however, there is a return to the movie star profile. I suppose people like reading about them. I know I do, even though I don't believe half of what I read. I myself have been interviewed at intervals over the years, in America, England, Italy, France, Mexico, Cuba, Panama, South America. I have often been misquoted and sometimes made to sound like a jackass. I can sympathize with Warren Beatty when he says, as he did to me, "I don't mind if they make me out a bastard. I just don't want them to make me out an idiot." This is why I try to be accurate when I write about people. Fortunately, I have a terrific memory, the tool of my trade, so that I never use a tape recorder, which would only inhibit me. I have a reputation for quoting people accurately.

Warren is one of the stars I liked best, a runner-up to Michael Caine, along with Marcello Mastroianni, Mick Jagger, Peter Fonda, Peter Finch, Robert Mitchum, Calvin Lockhart. They are, or were, all people who talk intelligently about subjects other than films. There have been a few stars to whom I couldn't talk at all and I didn't try. I went to see Natalie Wood in her suite at the Plaza and I sensed right off the bat that I couldn't write about her. She was a Hollywood child actress grown up to be a Hollywood star, and I knew I couldn't break through her practiced interview persona. Lee Remick was another. She was polite, even rather pleasant in a restrained way, but also, at least to me, uninteresting. Frankly, she bored me. I admired Jean Gabin's films, but when I met him, the person who introduced us effectively killed the act by explaining that I had written *Latins Are Lousy Lovers*: *"Elle est la dame qui a écrit 'Les Latins sont les amants horribles.'"* Her French was bad but not bad enough to be incomprehensible. Monsieur Gabin looked as if someone had dumped a live basilisk in his lap. *"Ah, oui?"* he said coldly, and promptly got up and walked off. Anyway, he was very short and had an unfortunate resemblance to Nelson Eddy—quite different from his screen image.

Then there was the dimpled and auriculate Clark Gable. I was never a Gable fan, although as a film critic I saw many of his pictures. (I thought *Gone with the Wind* was a sappy soap opera.) During a Hollywood trip in 1956, it was arranged for me to visit him on the set of a movie he was making with Eleanor Parker. I watched him rehearse an entrance scene some dozen times, flubbing his lines. During a lull, the press agent brought him over to where I sat and introduced him, The King, in person. He stood there, looking down at me, and I sat there, looking up at him. It was apparent that neither of us could think of anything to say. I guess he was waiting for me to begin. Finally, I said, "My little girl has a friend whose mother, Mrs. Popovich, is crazy about you."

And Clark Gable said to me: "Oh." Then the director called him, he went back to the set and I went away.

Chapter Twelve

OUR GIRL IN HAVANA

It was J. P. McEvoy who first persuaded me to go to Havana. His Christian names were Joseph Patrick, but he used only the initials. His friends called him Mac. Short and stocky, with a halo of wiry gray hair, he had a kinetic energy that was manifested in a gusto for life and an eclectic curiosity.

He wrote short stories for magazines like *The Saturday Evening Post*, the words and lyrics for at least one Broadway revue and the so-called plot line for a comic strip called "Dixie Dugan." He had a place in Woodstock, New York, at that time a well-known artists and writers colony. His main house and guest house were seldom empty, especially on summer weekends. There was a great deal of to-ing and fro-ing between bedrooms, somewhat less than secretive because the floor boards of both houses creaked loudly at even a tiptoe. We drank gallons of applejack, danced in Mac's barn to phonograph records on a wind-up Victrola, assuaged our hangovers the next morning with Prohibition bootleg beer and then lolled around his pool, the girls with toenails painted to match fingernails and lips. In the Thirties painted toenails were *de rigueur*, so much so that one female guest remarked to me about an aristocratic-looking young woman, "She can't be sleeping with men because she doesn't wear any toenail polish." We had read Joseph Moncure March's *The Wild Party*, in which he described a girl who was "swell to sleep with. Her toenails were scarlet. She looked like and had been a Mexican harlot."

At the house there would always be Mac's sweetheart, a softly pretty, pliant, amiable Polish girl. The guests were usually more or less celebrated people. Mickey Hahn—Emily Hahn, author, geologist, traveler—came one weekend when I was there. She had a beautiful face and a brilliant mind. "They call her 'Honeypot Hahn' because the men swarm around her like bees," commented Nancy Hale, the novelist, rather acidulously. That particular weekend Mickey had in tow a dazzlingly intelligent young South African scientist. His name was Solly Zuckerman, although I never called him anything but Baby. He had written a book with a title that S. J. Perelman might have thought up: *The Menstrual Cycle of the Sub-Human Primate, with Especial Reference to the Chacma Baboon.* He had come from London to continue his research at Yale on a Rockefeller grant. We had a brief affair, more intellectual than passionate, which began in Woodstock and continued other weekends in New York. (I particularly remember that he used to be impressed by how well I looked when he woke up beside me, unaware that in those days I used to stagger out of bed in the early morning, wash my face and renew my make-up and then creep back in bed.) Today, he is Lord Zuckerman, for many years chief scientific adviser to the British government, now a revered and hallowed elder statesman of science. I still have his youthful letters to me.

McEvoy, it turned out, was a dedicated Cuba buff, as were the author Manuel Komroff, the painter Bernard Karfiol, the architect and designer Paul Frankl, publisher Max Schuster, directors Josh Logan and John Huston, playwright Tom Heggen, Frances Steloff, who ran the Gotham Book Mart, and others whom I was to meet in the course of our shared love affair with Havana. McEvoy, in fact, later went to live there as Cuban representative of *Reader's Digest*, a sinecure with a huge salary, although he spoke no Spanish and, as far as I know, never wrote a word about Cuba. He and his last wife, Peggy, lived like Kublai Khan in a luxurious mansion with a platoon of butlers, maids and gardeners.

It was on one of the Woodstock weekends that Mac insisted that I go to Havana. I was considering Bermuda for a vacation but he said he was sure I would be as crazy about Havana as he was. He added that he had a good friend there, Jim Kendrigan, the American athletic coach at the University of Havana, who would show me around. Kendrigan was the guide, mentor and much-loved friend of all the aforementioned Cuba *aficionados*. When I agreed to go, Mac cabled Kendrigan, who cabled back that he would be happy to take me under his wing. At the end of January 1933, I sailed on the Cunard ship *Franconia* for a ten-day cruise with one day in Nassau and three in Havana. On board with their wives were 160 delegates to a druggists' convention, assorted bigwigs of businesses that supply drugstores, Governor Joseph Ely of Massachusetts, Edna Woolman Chase, editor in chief of *Vogue*, and a couple of congressmen.

There was also a swarthy little man who looked like a Sicilian gangster, talked like one and, indeed, turned out to be one. He took a fancy to me and followed me around the ship, although he never made a pass or stepped out of line. I didn't see him in Havana but on the voyage back he presented me with a large bottle of Guerlain's L'Heure Bleu, the biggest bottle of perfume I had ever had, and made me a surprising proposition. "You've got class," he said. "You could teach me to talk good English and how to act in a swell restaurant and stuff like that. How about it?" I turned down this tutorial post. Some time later I read in a newspaper that he was indicted for income tax evasion, along with Johnny Torrio, the multimillionaire Mafia boss who had gone from Brooklyn to head the Chicago rackets after World War I, taking with him Al Capone as his lieutenant. The newspaper report called Torrio "Public Enemy No. 1" and said that my admirer was a henchman of his and "a political power in New Jersey." It added that he had been questioned in the Lindbergh baby kidnap-murder case. I never heard of him again. I wondered if he ever went back to Havana. It was his first trip there and, like me, he had fallen in love with that magic city.

The *Franconia* docked in Havana on February 1, 1933. Kendrigan was there to meet me and we began a close, but platonic, friendship that was to last for twenty years. He was an extraordinary man, a lapsed Dominican scholar and Catholic seminarian, with a wry, perverse sense of humor, given to Latin and Greek quotations. Originally from New England, he opened a private school for problem boys in Biloxi, Mississippi, about the time

Alexander Neill started a similar experimental school, Sum-
merhill, which became world-famous and is still flourishing in
England. Kendrigan's school petered out in 1925 and he went to
Havana to teach Latin at the University there but switched to director of athletics and unorthodox coach of football, basketball
and track. (He gave his students fanciful names, like the Saint
Aloysius Total Abstinence Basketball Team, and fed them dex-
trose.) From the very first, he was seduced by the hypnotic lotus-
eater ambiance of Havana the sorceress. He abandoned his wife
and child in America and never went back there until he was an
old man, sick unto death, blinded by cataracts. His wife, summoned by the American Embassy, went to Cuba and took him
back to her home in Peoria, where he died. He would have been
furious if he had known, but McEvoy, who visited him during his
last days, reported that he thought he was still in Havana.

When I met him, he was in his early fifties. He lived a life of
sensuous hedonism, surrounded by young Cuban girls of assorted
shades, who were variously described as "my laundress," "my
seamstress," "my secretary," "my masseuse," "my language student." I remember many of them, especially one whose mother
had named her Essolena after the gas station signs. Kendrigan
called her Gladys and said he was teaching her English, but all
she could say was "See my pink tongue," suiting the action to the
words.

He was always short of money and when the university was
closed because of political ferment, as it frequently was, he eked
out a living for himself and his entourage by acting as a benign,
humorously lewd cicerone to visitors sent by McEvoy, and attempting unsuccessful enterprises such as smuggling gold by
means of old ladies, until he ran out of old ladies, or trying to
raise capital to finance Cuban handicrafts.

I learned more about him on subsequent trips but at first sight
he seemed a respectable elderly professorial type. I was totally
unprepared for the giddy merry-go-round that followed our initial
drinks at the Lucero, a little sidewalk bar overlooking the Male-
con and the sea, where he introduced me to the *mojito criollo*,
white rum with a touch of vermouth and a mintlike leaf called
yerba buena. He talked to me courteously, questioning me about
Mac, about my work on *Vanity Fair* magazine, about the boat

trip. Finally he looked at his watch. "Do you like movies?" he asked. "Oh yes, I love movies," I replied innocently. "Well," he said, "it's too early to go to a nightclub. Let's go to a movie to kill time."

So off we went to the Teatro Shanghai, where he bought seats in a box. It wasn't until I put on my glasses that I realized I was the only woman in the audience, which was mostly Chinese. The picture had already started and when I looked at the screen it was evident that I was seeing my first blue movie. Kendrigan's face was expressionless. I wasn't going to let him know how startled I was, so I watched as calmly as if I were seeing Mary Pickford in *Daddy Long Legs*. Remember, this was forty-five years ago, before nudity and explicit sex became run-of-the-mill cinematic staples. Actually, the movie was hilarious because it was an old silent "stag party" film, made with fast, jerky movements. The men wore Boston garters on their socks and the women wore camisoles and corsets. They threw off their clothes at top speed, the men keeping on socks and garters, and then it was all double-quick run run, jump jump, fuck fuck, suck suck, with the film flickering crazily like Keystone Kops slapstick. The audience kept shouting helpful suggestions at strategic parts, and I began to laugh and couldn't stop. I doubt if it was the reaction Kendrigan expected.

Looking back, I don't see how we managed to cram so much into three nights and days, but we did: nightclubs, taxi dance-halls, brothels, waterfront bars, music halls, jai alai games, cock-fights, countryside trips, private parties. I slept hardly at all and went back to the ship only to take a catnap, bathe and change clothes. The music, the drinking, the wonderful Cuban air teeming with ardent softness—all blended into an atmosphere of sultry enticement, at once stimulating and relaxing. I could drink straight rum for fourteen consecutive hours, sleep for an hour or so and wake up with a head as clear as a bell. One reason I've always enjoyed drinking anywhere is that it gives me "Dutch courage." I can talk freely to people, without inhibiting self-consciousness, and this makes me feel popular and confident. In Cuba I could drink night and day without ever getting tired or sick or hungry or sloppy. The more I drank, the more fluent my Spanish became, the brighter my eyes, the more sure my step. I could even dance better.

When the *Franconia* sailed out of Havana harbor I stood at the rail with tears in my eyes, but I was happy because I knew that I would return. I was in love, not with any man, but with the city. I wanted to live there. I wanted to die there. I still do.

During later visits I soon learned that beneath the surface glitter of vice, the tourist playground glamour, there was a constant inner turmoil caused by desperate poverty, starvation wages and hideously brutal oppression, aided and abetted by the United States. There were always brave Cubans fighting against this tyrannical exploitation but they were hunted down, tortured, garroted, shot or thrown live to the sharks through a trap door in Morro fortress. The good old days for the tourists were the bad old days for the majority of Cubans. It was the time of *las vacas gordas*, the fat cows. (We call them fat cats.) There was more graft and corruption to the square inch, relatively, than in any other country, all under the auspices of United States financial interests supported by successive American governments. Cuba was an appendage of Wall Street.

On my first trip the dictator was Gerardo Machado, who overthrew the constitution, closed the civil courts, put an end to free speech, denied the right of public assembly and shut the university, throwing five thousand students into the streets. Doctors, lawyers, professors, editors, anyone who whispered against him, were killed in their homes, on the streets or in jail. He was called "The Man of a Thousand Murders," but he was publicly praised by our ambassador at the time.

In May 1934, shortly after my third visit, he was overthrown in a military revolt led by the mulatto sergeant Fulgencio Batista. The horror and the corruption continued. "The thefts of the Batista regime run not into millions but billions," wrote Carleton Beals, a long-time Cuba observer. Beals estimated that when Batista fled the country in 1959, his personal take alone was more than $400 million. It had been a similar story from the turn of the century. One Minister of Education simply drove up to the official bank with a bunch of suitcases. When the guard asked him what he wanted he said he had come to get some money and laughed. So the guard laughed, too, and the Minister went into the bank with his aides and all the suitcases and scooped up money, then drove to the airport. When he died a few years later

in Miami, it was reported in the New York *Times* that he left a
fortune of $300 million. And he was only Minister of Education.
The Ministers of Public Works did even better. The graft, known
as *la mordida*, the bite, extended all the way down the line—
mayors, police chiefs, small-time officials—while the workers and
peasants went hungry.

I was in Havana in March 1935, when the underground movement called a general strike. The government clamped down.
Meetings of more than three persons were forbidden and anyone
on the streets after 9 P.M. was shot on sight. A cannon went off at
9 and if we were still sitting at a sidewalk café, we all got up and
ran. I was spending my time with Kendrigan and his friend Mercedes Luks, the Cuban widow of George Luks, the painter. She
was then in her thirties and looked like a young Merle Oberon,
slim, with long, satiny black hair, black Etruscan eyes—Luks used
to call them "the antique eyes of Mercedes"—and when she
talked she flamed with an exciting vitality until she seemed to
throw off sparks.

We three were a constant trio. On the night before the general
strike began, we were drinking at a café on the Prado. That afternoon the army had taken over the university and stationed soldiers like a chain around the grounds. Bombs had gone off in the
customshouse and in several other government buildings. The
wings of terror quivered over the city and gave a toxic, expectant
quality to the air. "This is our last night out," Kendrigan said.
"Havana will be under martial law tomorrow. You're going to see
trouble this visit." I leaned my elbows on the table and made a
face. "Listen," I said recklessly. "I am going to get so stinking
drunk that if there's shooting going on I won't believe it. I've
been yellow all my life and I'm not going to start making gallant
poses now." I called the waiter with the customary hiss, "Psst!"
When he came over, I told him to bring three *mojitos*. He nodded and started away. "See what the rest of the folks will have," I
shouted. "Those three are for me."

By the time we left the café and reached the Miami Cabaret
the bridge of my nose felt like cold marble. I kept pinching it but
there was no feeling there. Mercedes was getting voluble about
her liver, discussing it with the same nervous frenzy she had
shown in talking about the strike. "I don't know why it is," she

rattled on, "but my God, we Latins have such terrible livers. That's why we can't drink. It's awful. I can't drink a thing." "For anyone who can't drink a thing you seem to be doing nicely," Kendrigan said in his quiet, even tone. "That's right," Mercedes cried. "Go ahead and insult me. You see how he treats me? My God, what I endure! Why do I stand for it?" "Probably because you love to suffer," Kendrigan said, with a secret smile twitching at the corners of his mouth. "Suffering is a luxury of Latin women." "May your mother's womb be eaten by a barracuda!" she screamed in Spanish. "My mother's womb was eaten by cemetery worms long ago in Biloxi, Mississippi," he said calmly.

This dour badinage was interrupted by an American tourist who got up from the next table and lurched over to us. "Say!" he bellowed. "You people are Americans, or some of you are." "No," said Mercedes. "We are three escaped lunatics, as any idiot could tell." A look of confusion dimmed the tourist's ruddy face but he rallied himself and bowed to me with painstaking regard for his balance. "Would you care to dance with me?" "It is all that I need to fulfill me," I said, not too brightly, "but first you must ask my grandfather." I nodded at Kendrigan, who rose and bowed. "The bells of hell ring ting-a-ling-a-ling for me but not for you," he said, and sat down. "What bells?" asked the tourist. "I don't get you." "Neither do you get the young lady. In fact, nobody gets her. She is the Antigone for whom all men long." The tourist retreated hastily to his own table. "I do think he might have put up a fight for me," I said. "If you won't let me pick up men, at least buy me another drink." "I will not buy you another drink because we are going to my house where Mercedes can nurse her Latin liver and you and I can drink in peace because tomorrow we will probably be shot as innocent bystanders."

We took a taxi to Kendrigan's crumbling stone house with its massive carved mahogany doors facing the sea. On the way we were stopped twice by soldiers who searched the taxi for bombs or firearms. They also searched the driver and us. "From the way they search me," Mercedes complained, "they must think I carry bombs in the most peculiar place."

When we reached the house, there were two Cubans waiting. Jim introduced them as José and his wife, Consuela. Then he and the man went into another room to talk. The wife sat primly on her chair, small and plump and disapproving. She refused a drink. Mercedes poured one for me and then lay down on a couch and moaned about her liver. "Oh, fuck my liver," she suddenly exploded. "Will no one get me a drink? I might as well die this way as be blown to bits by a bomb. Listen, Helen, if that drink is for me, I'm not an orphan. Well, I am, but never mind. You can fill it up."

The two men came back in the room. José was very tall for a Cuban. There were scars on his thin face that gave him a slightly sinister look, but his mouth was beautiful. His eyes were strange. At first I couldn't understand what made them so distrubing but then I realized that they were of different colors, one blue, one green. He kept staring at me with a look that was diamond-hard, diamond-bright, with something shining so sharply that I turned my face away. In five visits to Havana, he was the first Cuban to whom I felt sexually attracted.

When he left with the woman, Kendrigan, who called him The Killer, told me that he was a doctor and a member of a secret rebel organization known as the ABC. "He makes little bombs by putting explosive in cigarette boxes. You know those blue cardboard boxes of your favorite cigarettes Partagas *y nada mas?* He has been in prison but so far they haven't shot him. He was hiding here tonight because the soldiers searched his house today and found dynamite, gunpowder, a machine gun and a rifle. I can see that you like him and that he likes you. If we all survive, I'll arrange a clandestine meeting." "Never mind," I said. "You're lying. You must be lying. I'm going back to my hotel. This is all too much for me. No, don't come with me. It's only three blocks and I'll be safe. Remember, I'm an American tourist. I guess I've been acting like one, too. See you *mañana.* I hope."

My room was on the *azotea* of a small hotel on the Prado. That is to say, it was a tiny place on the roof, dignified by the name of penthouse but really just a little wooden shack with bedroom and bathroom. The elevator boy who took me up wore a revolver in a holster strapped to his waist. "Lotsa trouble," he said cheerfully. When we reached the roof I started out of the elevator but he stopped me. "Wait." He pointed to three long rays of light which were playing on the roofs and balconies all along the street. "Antiaircraft searchlights." For a moment the three rays switched to the hotel roof, illuminating every corner with a strong white light. "They see person on roof, they shoot," the boy said. "Soldiers have machine guns in street. They shoot revolutionaries on roofs. You no go on roof. Maybe they make mistake, shoot you." He laughed in his chipper way, looking like a bright-eyed squirrel. Then, as the lights slanted toward another direction, he gave me a slight push. "All right. Go now. Quick!" He closed the elevator door with a bang and was gone, as I ran across the roof and into my room.

I undressed quickly and got into bed. Although I had closed the shutters I could see the searchlights flashing through them. They made bright patterns on the walls and floor, like some strange, unreal moonlight. I sat up in bed and watched them. When the first shots came, a sharp, cracking sound, three, four, five of them, then silence again, I was too chilled with fear to move. It was only a moment before they began again, and this time I jumped from bed and stood in my bare feet on the tile floor. I felt as if a circle of ice had congealed around my heart. I could hear the bullets richochet against the roof that surrounded my room. My impulse was to get under the bed and cower there, but then I thought, "How awful if a bullet hit me and I was found *under* the bed!" So I climbed back in and lit a cigarette. Sleep was impossible amid the quick, spitting explosion of the shots and their impact, stopping briefly, then beginning again, while the searchlights continued to sweep the roof. To steady myself I tried to remember the long poems I used to learn in school to speak before the class. I started on "The Deacon's Masterpiece or The Wonderful One Hoss Shay" but got stuck at the line " 'Huddup!' said the parson. Off went they," and had to change to Tennyson's "Ode on the Death of the Duke of Wellington." Eventually the shots seemed to have shifted to neighboring rooftops and I fell asleep.

The next day the general strike was on and martial law was proclaimed, but Kendrigan, ever the satyr manipulator of other people's sex lives, managed to contact José, who knocked at my door in the afternoon. He was the first Cuban I ever slept with. Our mating was scarcely a wild success, accompanied as it was by the maid clattering her mop and broom outside my room and the sound of gunfire in the street. Afterward, we went to Kendrigan's house where I confided in Jim that José had a long, thin, stiletto-type penis. Jim was fascinated by this information and eager to further the alliance, a difficult project in view of the political situation. Furthermore, we were joined at Jim's by Luis Alfredo López-Méndez, a Venezuelan exile who worked as a commercial artist for El Encanto department store. His father was in prison back home for having participated in a revolt against Juan Vicente Gómez, dictator of Venezuela for the previous twenty-five years, a lecherous tyrant who was rumored to have sired hundreds of illegitimate children.

The results of my introduction to López-Méndez had elements of a Feydeau farce or a Cuban version of *Up in Mabel's Room*. He had recently divorced his wife, who had run away with his best friend. The friend, piling Ossa on Pelion, also borrowed Luis Alfredo's overcoat and suitcase. Havana was a gossip monger's paradise, so I knew about the elopement before he did, as he thought his friend had gone to Mexico on a business trip and that his wife was visiting her mother. This was the year before I met him. Anyway, for the few days of the strike, Jim, Mercedes, The Killer, López-Méndez and I were all holed up in Jim's house. What with the tension, the bombs, the rum and a touch of transient insanity, López-Méndez asked me to marry him, without any preliminary courtship, and I guess I must have more or less accepted him without taking it seriously.

Meanwhile, the American papers carried reports of the strike, the bombs and gunfire. Condé Nast telephoned the State Department in Washington, and my editor, Frank Crowninshield, cabled the American ambassador in Havana, seeking reassurance as to my safety. A few days after the strike was crushed, passage home was arranged for me on the Ward Line ship the *Morro Castle*. The day I left I brought my bags over to Jim's place for a hectic farewell. I was in a bedroom with The Killer while López-Méndez lurked suspiciously in the living room and Mercedes and Kendrigan tried to distract him. The five of us drove to the ship with a trio of musicians playing "Adiós, Compañeros de Mi Vida," and we all wept.

When the ship arrived in New York, I was met by my mother and two of my friends, both Condé Nast employees who were anxious to ask me about Cuba but didn't get a chance. My garrulous mother immediately launched into an account of a dinner she had attended the evening before my arrival. "It started with a fruit cup—well, you couldn't really call it a fruit cup—it had melon and pineapple and shrimp. . . ." She prattled on and on, all the way to my apartment. It never used to enter her head that other people were not spellbound by her persistent accounts of what she ate, which took precedence over all other subjects. It didn't occur to her to ask me about events in Havana.

I went back to work on *Vanity Fair* and sent Kendrigan a cable, *Ave etque vale*, but followed it with a series of letters saying I was determined to return to Cuba as soon as possible. López-Méndez had gone deep-sea fishing off the Florida Keys with Ernest Hemingway and John Dos Passos. Hemingway advised him not to marry me, saying I was too complex for him, but Dos Passos told him to go ahead. He relayed this news in a letter and announced that he was coming to New York for the wedding.

Meanwhile, Kendrigan wrote me: "Your letters confuse me and they excited Mercedes so much she went mad for an hour and bought perfume, a feather duster, pink toilet paper and Ovid's *Art of Love* . . . . The Killer is out of danger and has been promoted, I suppose because he was not arrested and shot. This is Alice in Wonderland country. *Felix potuit rerum cognoscere causas*. He came to the house and said he has written you. I found him poring over my collection of erotica so he may be preparing a new type of message. He tells me he does not love Consuela but does not know what to do with her. She is enamored of his stiletto. He says he has a lot in store for you so you might bring a flying trapeze with your other more prosaic belongings. I hope you will (1) get a month's leave of absence instead of quitting your job; (2) take the precaution to marry Condé Nast before you leave; or (3) agree to accept advice and counsel from him before doing anything rash. . . . López-Méndez is hopeful. *Tarde fué tomado Troy, pero fué tomado.* [Troy was taken late, but it was taken.] I am still Pontius Pilate as to your decision. Love and sympathy, Jim."

López-Méndez arrived in New York and stayed with me for a week, ending in a tequila haze during which we were married at the Judson Memorial Baptist Church in Greenwich Village, a comic operetta affair as he spoke no English and I had to interpret. I think my motivation was that I desperately wanted to live in Havana and this seemed at the time, what with the tequila, a not too unreasonable solution.

The news hit the Havana papers and also American ones. Most of the accounts led off with "Following a whirlwind courtship." Uh-huh. I sent my bridegroom to Havana, promising to join him as soon as I could wind up things in New York. Condé, who had been asking me to marry him for several years, off and on, was angry with me, and everyone else was surprised, puzzled, disbelieving or upset in varying degrees.

Before the wedding I had been receiving florid love letters in Spanish from José ("I hope that soon, like the birds that emigrate in the spring, you will return to Cuba . . . that your soul remains poised like a tigress wishing to leap, and in this manner I want you to leap on me, with the possessive fever of your mouth. . . . Drink a rum as if it were a liquid kiss from your Cuban love," and so on). But now, he wrote me in English: "My dear Lady: I feel a shock of surprise seeing how your mind elaborates so many differents sentiments and morbids forms of love. As a doctor I analyze you. In love you have like a modern American Siva many arms. Why in heavens name did López-Méndez commit marriage with you? Well now I lose my humor in writing this letter to a girl who is clever in her regular life and then is so dumb-bell in such a simple matter. You are nut!! Excuse the contrast between the last romantic letter and this one. It is in account of your conduct. Though I wait for you with sadistic desire. Kisses, Joe."

A flurry of letters continued during the next few months. From Kendrigan: "I am really upset. You must not come here to live. You must hold onto your job. I want you to return many times but not to break up your future. You must drink more and more milk and quiet down. Be a good girl and don't get reckless."

I wrote The Killer a letter in care of Jim. After he read it, he left it in Jim's desk for safekeeping and López-Méndez, looking for some writing paper, found it and read it. He tore it in pieces and sent them to me. Kendrigan wrote me about the incident, adding that he was trying to placate him. "He is very angry with you but I told him the way is to forget about it. He is a complete wreck and is taking cocaine and has bought a gun and says he will shoot you if you come here. He accused me of witchcraft, using love philtres, etc. As for The Killer, he is badly upset. His pride is

severely hurt by your marriage. He thinks you were drugged or hyp-
notized. In fact, he was hauling you over the coals yesterday
morning in a loud voice when López-Méndez rang my bell and
demanded to be let in. The Killer went out the window and
jumped off the balcony in a decided huff. Luis Alfredo came in
and said, 'Who was shouting?' and I said it was one of my students and he said, 'It certainly sounded like that cross-eyed doctor,' so I had to laugh. He isn't cross-eyed, as you know. He has a
nice blue eye. Anyway, you must get this tangled mess straightened out. When you come here you will have to behave. For my
part I feel like Dr. Frankenstein and not a bit like Aretino. So you
must be a good girl here, at least in public. Your husband is well
known and well liked. I am still convinced the proper thing would
be for you to live with him until it becomes impossible. He is a
lot better when he doesn't start expressing himself. There is no
doubt you would not be as bored by him here as in New York. I
am so damned puzzled about it all. I can come to no sensible con-
clusion about you. Maybe you should get a divorce and have Luis
Alfredo and The Killer as your lovers, but that wouldn't work out,
as Luis would not share you. I will get out my old dust-covered
Ouija board and talk it over with myself. You are as a matter of
fact a very bad child but a very special one. P.S. I am trying to
find the Havana newspaper report of your marriage. I think Mercedes ate it in her first moments of shock."

From me to Kendrigan: "Well well well. It looks as if the in-
domitable Mrs. Norden has gone and fucked things up for fair.
Will you kindly explain how I ever got myself into all this mess? I
remember saying, with a faintly superior sniff of disdain, that I
would never become involved in any of your fine, devious Havana
intrigues. Was it the ambiance? Or a general crumbling of my
mental fiber? And now how do I get out? I realize how much happier I was when you and I wandered around in peaceful fraternity.
I don't blame you for feeling like Frankenstein. Why weren't we
content to keep me always the observer? I am sorry you have to
bear the brunt of it all but I love the idea of José leaping over the
balcony. Haven't he and Luis Alfredo met face to face? I can just
see myself in Havana leading a life of tortuous intrigue, dashing
secretly in and out of doorways, draped in black veil, writing in in-
visible ink and getting my nose shot off by jealous husbands or

wives. I was always such a simple, open girl. Well, open, anyway.
I don't want to go to Havana and find a flock of new-laid enemies. I still don't know what is best to do. However, I feel—and I
may be struck dead for my smugness—that I will be all right no
matter what happens."

From me to Kendrigan again: "Surely you must know, without
being told, that I am not the least bit in love with López-Méndez.
I am mildly fond of him and I think he is frequently amusing,
sometimes unconsciously. These are the things against the marriage: that I don't love him; that he is so jealous that I may get in
a mess or even shot; that I am still slightly infatuated with José;
that I am used to utter freedom and independence and am not
easily bossed around; that I will not go fishing with Dos Passos
and Hemingway or with anyone else because I hate fishing, get
seasick, and am scared of small boats on the ocean. On the other
hand, in favor of the marriage: that he is, or at least seems to be
at present, in love with me; that he is likable and fairly intelligent
and sophisticated; that as long as I am determined to come to
Havana to live it would be nice to have him help me; that he in-
sists I must not work and that he will support me, although I earn
as much in a week as he does in a month, so one could hardly say
I married for money. . . If I thought I could have The Killer, I
would urge Luis Alfredo to get a divorce immediately. But if I got
José, then what would I do with him? Only one thing is certain.
Havana, the city, means more to me than the whole kit and
caboodle put together. I will pray to Saint Lazarus and maybe I
will be shown the way."

In the end, López-Méndez got a Cuban divorce on the grounds
of desertion and quickly married a girl named Aida Jesús something, who ran the elevator in El Encanto store. I met him once
on the street after I went to live in Cuba. Instead of shooting me,
he embraced me fervently and begged me to have a drink with
him. "I am so bored," he complained. Some time later, Gómez
died, Luis Alfredo's father was let out of prison and the family
money and estate were restored. Luis Alfredo took Aida Jesús and
went back to Venezuela, where he became director of the National Museum, then Minister of Culture in the government and,
later, his country's consul in Paris. The last I heard of him, over
twenty years ago, he was a senator in Venezuela. After I married

Jack Lawrenson, I had a chatty letter from him, full of family news: His son was attending military school in Peekskill, New York; his daughter by his first wife was married; etc. He ended by saying, "Regards to Mr. Lawrenson," whom he had never met. Jack and I named one of our cats after him, but it was embarrassing to call "Luis Alfredo! Luis Alfredo!" at night in our Greenwich Village back garden when the cat had gone over the fence. Windows in neighboring apartment buildings would open and heads pop out, so we shortened his name to Fred. He got the mange and had to be put down.

I went back to Havana a dozen or more times, including twice with Jack, who loved the city as much as I did and who appreciated Kendrigan, and twice after Fidel came to power, when I took my children there to see the new, liberated Cuba. But all that is another story.

Chapter Thirteen

FROM CHERRY BOUNCE TO
VIPER BRANDY

Some years ago I was looking in the window of a New York antiques shop. In the center of the display was a pair of men's cuff links on a small velvet cushion, with a white card on which was printed in ink: *Antique cufflinks. Circa 1907.* That was the year I was born. Antique, indeed. "Faugh!" I said to myself, or would have said if I had any idea how to pronounce it. The incident reminded me of when my daughter was about nine and a peanut butter addict. I remarked that when I was a child I, too, loved peanut butter. She looked at me in astonishment and exclaimed, "Did they have peanut butter that long ago?"

It doesn't seem long ago to me. I guess it never does. Irwin Shaw once told me that he was sure that when he's dying at the age of ninety-two he'll think, "This is ridiculous. This can't happen to a baby like me." Still, I must admit that nowadays when I read in a magazine reminiscences of a writer's childhood back in the old days and these "old days" turn out to be the Fifties, I begin to feel slightly like some mammoth that has been dug intact out of the ice in Siberia or Ultima Thule, a quirkily preserved remnant of another age. Most of my acquaintances, friends and lovers of yesteryear are dead. Even my former doctors, dentists and oculists are either dead or retired. I scan the newspaper obituary pages, something I never used to do, and I look at the ages even of those people of whom I've never heard. I'm delighted when they were in their nineties. I myself plan to live to the year 2000 but I can't bank on it. While I can still remember, I like to think back to what it was to be a child in the early part of the century and to trace the route that led from LaFargeville, an upstate New York village of four hundred inhabitants, to the more sophisticated fleshpots of New York City, Paris, London, Rome, Havana, Madrid and other metropolitan capitals where I have lived.

The house my grandmother built was the first in the village to have electric lights. She bought the fixtures in New York at Sloane's, who sent a man up to LaFargeville to supervise the installation. Other people used kerosene lamps and candles, as we did in our summer place on the St. Lawrence River. At one period, when I began to hate my Indian-straight hair, which I wore in what was called a Dutch bob or a Buster Brown, I used to try to curl it with iron curling tongs which I heated by holding them down the chimney of a kerosene lamp and then unsuccessfully attempted to crimp my locks into a marcelle wave. When I was older I had a "permanent" in Syracuse, a frightening experience in those days, as your hair was rolled around dozens of metal things suspended by wires from a central machine like a Charles Addams chandelier. Then the electricity was turned on and there you sat, unable to move your head, hitched to this torture instrument for an hour or more. There were quite a few cases where women had their hair burned off.

We always had an inside toilet, a complete bathroom both in LaFargeville and later in the summer house, but I was certainly familiar with other people's wooden outhouses, or privies, unheated and pretty chilly in winter, which was why everyone kept a chamber pot under the bed. (We had sets of pots, slop jars, pitchers, wash bowls, soap dishes and shaving mugs, all in china hand-painted with floral patterns.) I remember especially a neighbor's three-seater family privy with large, medium and small holes, and old Sears, Roebuck catalogues for toilet paper. When my mother was a child there were no inside toilets at all. A dirty joke of that era was a riddle: "Come, little riddle-cum-riss, what is it a boy takes hold of when he goes out to piss?" Answer: "The door knob." That was supposed to be a scream. One of the many things that impress me about today's young generation is that they don't tell dirty jokes. My mother's generation told them exuberantly and so did mine. They still do. I don't know a single young person today who tells dirty jokes or who would think them funny. I can't imagine them splitting their sides over the mere mention of cloacal or genital terms, as we did and our parents did. We grew up, and our parents before us, taught that natural bodily functions, including sex, were dirty, unmentionable, and at the same time, by some curious perversity, hilarious when referred to in "risqué" jokes.

All public places in our county's villages and towns, such as railway stations, stores, hotels, post offices and many private houses, too, had cuspidors, less elegantly called spittoons, celebrated by the local children with a song that went, to the tune from *Carmen*: "Toreador-a, don't spit on the floor-a. Use the cuspidor-a; that's what it is for-a." Most public places were heated by potbellied iron stoves. In our LaFargeville house we had a coal furnace and a large granite fireplace. We cooked on a big black iron kitchen range with round lids on top that had indentations into which you hooked an iron lid-lifter in order to remove the lid to shovel in more coal or throw in wood. For ironing we used black flatirons, heated on the stove top. (Wrapped in a towel, they also served to warm the beds on cold nights.) The washing was done in corrugated tin tubs with wringers made of two rolls of hard rubber, turned by a handle, and washboards on which we scrubbed the clothes. My grandmother and I sometimes did this work, even though we had a maid, called the hired girl, who lived in a big room at the top of the house and ate with us in the kitchen, except when my mother was there. Then the family ate in the dining room with its solid mahogany furniture, petit-point seat covers on the chairs, a silver tea set on a side table and an oriental rug under which was a buzzer in front of the chair at the head of the table. When my mother visited us, she always sat there and she liked to press her foot on the buzzer to bring the hired girl running from the kitchen through the butler's pantry (as it was called, although we certainly had no butler) and bursting open the swinging door into the dining room. My grandmother obviously thought this was a lot of folderol but she put up with it because she never crossed my mother. Not many people did.

One of my treats was when my grandmother would take me up

to the depot (pronounced *dee-po*, accent on the first syllable) to
watch the "flyer" rush through, a terrifying black monster, its
whistle going full blast. It scared me but I enjoyed it. I have always loved trains and still prefer them to ship or plane. There
were only two trains that stopped at our little wooden depot: the
daily milk train and a local train that stopped when the station-
master stood near the track and waved a red flag at it. We took
the latter train when we went to other villages or to Watertown,
the nearest town where we could change to the flyer if we were
going to visit my parents in Syracuse. All trains carried a brake-
man, whose job was to get out first at a station and put on the
ground a stool for passengers to step on. The trains also had an
iron contraption on the front of the engine, called a cow catcher.
They sometimes caught them, too, when some unfortunate bossy
strayed onto the tracks.

During our Syracuse visits, an even more thrilling adventure
was to walk to the nearest fire engine house to watch the daily
hitch-up. This was a practice drill in which bells rang, firemen slid
down poles, hitched up the four horses to the red fire engine and
charged out, bells clanging, horses galloping, their tails and
manes flying. It was wonderfully exciting.

In springtime we went to the woods to pick trilliums and other
flowers; in the summer my grandmother made dandelion wine, el-
derberry wine and cherry bounce; in the autumn she put up
preserves and put down sauerkraut—I still don't understand the
adverbial difference but that's the way it was; and in the winter
she used to boil locally gathered maple syrup to make "wax" for
me. She filled a large enamel basin with clean snow, patted it
down hard, and poured the hot boiled syrup on it, making
designs, writing my name, drawing pictures of cats. It hardened
the minute it hit the snow and tasted delicious. I also liked the
cherry bounce, although she let me have only small sips. It was
sweet and sharp. My grandmother thought it warded off colds and
was good for the stomach. Sometimes I used to sneak into the
pantry and steal an extra, heady swig.

Our house on the St. Lawrence River is in a small community
on Wellesley Island whose year-round residents are referred to as
"the natives" by the summer people, although never by my grandmother who had no snobbish instincts, no racial or religious preju-

dices. The official name of the community, chosen by some laconic and not very imaginative early settler, is Fine View. Our house is on the riverbank and the boats pass in front of us, including the big foreign liners. The summer people live on the riverbank, and the year-round residents on the higher ground and in the rest of the island. Behind our house, on our part of what we called the hill, there was once a butternut tree, now gone. My grandmother used to bake molasses butternut cookies. It's a wonderful nut I've never come across in any other place or even heard of, with a large black shell, difficult to crack, but once you succeeded, the taste of the inner nut was better than pecans or almonds or Brazil nuts or any others.

We didn't have our hired girl summers, so when my parents were there I sometimes felt like Cinderella. I had to get up early in the morning and sweep the eel flies off the large veranda, do the dusting, wash down the stairs with a rag dipped in a small gray enamel basin of cold water and Gold Dust Twins soap powder, wield the wire rug-beater to beat the dust from rugs hung on the clothesline, go up the hill to get drinking water from a pump which I had to prime first, set the table, change the long strip of sticky flypaper that dangled over the kitchen table, covered with trapped insects, do the dishes, wind the Victrola and run errands, while my beautiful mother, smelling sweetly of Djer-Kiss and wearing a Japanese silk kimona, lay in the hammock issuing orders like Nelson at Trafalgar.

When my grandmother and I were there alone, I didn't have to do housework. We spent quiet afternoons sitting on the porch, watching the boats go by, playing Parcheesi, or reading out loud to each other. Sometimes she worked on embroidering linen towels for my hope chest, using an embroidery hoop, or making tatting lace to trim them, while I read out loud to her from Elbert Hubbard's Scrapbook. He was a disciple of William Morris, prone to epigrams, who went down on the *Lusitania*.

Frequently we took trips on the *Island Belle*, a side-wheeler (a boat with a paddle wheel amidships), or we went on shore dinners, picnics on deserted islands, with roasted corn on the cob and watermelon. Often we made ice cream in a galvanized iron utensil, the outside section packed with rock salt, turning the handle like mad for what seemed hours. We also went fishing for perch and black bass in our skiff, the *Lucy*, my grandmother and I taking turns at the oars. We didn't have any fancy gear, just poles with hooks on the end of a line, with wriggling earthworms for bait.

Evenings we sat on the porch until bedtime, watching the fireflies. I discovered that if I caught one and pressed its head, its tail would light up. We both slept in cots on the upstairs sleeping porch, wearing flannel nightgowns, with outing flannel nightcaps tied under our chins. Through the dark water of the river the ships passed almost silently in front of our house, on their way to and from the Great Lakes. Sometimes I awoke in the night and sat up in bed to watch them, beautiful and mysterious. If I caught a cold, my grandmother rubbed goose grease on my chest and covered it with a piece of warmed flannel. During the 1918 flu epidemic that killed twenty million people throughout the world, she sewed a lump of camphor into a small black silk bag, hung it on a ribbon around my neck and made me wear it night and day to protect me from the disease. When we went to Watertown to shop I had to wear a cheesecloth mask over my nose and mouth. I didn't mind because I loved going anywhere with her, especially into stores where the sales clerk put your money in a small metal box that then flew along an overhead wire near the ceiling till it reached the cashier on the balcony. The cashier opened the box, took out the money, put back the required change, and the box flew along the wire back down to the counter. It was a speedier operation than getting change in many big stores today.

My grandmother was religious but not overweeningly so. We went to church once in a while, if it wasn't raining, and we said our prayers together every night, not on our knees but comfortably in bed. Her father had been a Baptist minister. According to my mother, marijuana used to grow wild behind his LaFargeville church, although she refused to say if anyone took advantage of this. I doubt if my grandmother ever knew what it was. She disapproved of ordinary cigarettes and I never smoked in front of her, even though she was unorthodox in many ways. Still, she observed certain quaint conventions of the day. For example, after her husband died, she had all her silver jewelry oxidized, even her lorgnettes, a process that turned everything a dark gray, almost black. Then she never got around to having anything returned to the original state.

Actually, she wasn't my grandmother. She was my great-aunt by marriage. My mother's mother died of tuberculosis, then called galloping consumption, at the age of thirty-two. The older children went to live with different relatives, but my mother, who was three, was adopted by her father's brother and his wife, who were childless. The brother died before I was born, but his wife brought me up and I always considered her my grandmother. In fact, I thought of her more as my real mother, and I called her Ma. She was the only relative I loved and the only one who loved me. I lived with her during most of my childhood, until I went away to boarding school when I was nearly fifteen.

Extract from a letter my father wrote me on my fourth birthday: "Both Mama and Daddy are sorry they are not with you on this birthday of yours." From a letter on my fifth birthday: "Dear little daughter: Daddy wishes he could be with you but he is thinking of you." From a letter on my sixth birthday: "Daddy is sorry not to be with you on your birthday."

He only wrote on my birthdays and Christmas. My mother didn't write. My earliest memory of her is of her spanking me hard with a hairbrush. I was two and we were being photographed together in a Watertown studio. The photographer wanted me to stand on a bench beside her, put both my hands on her cheeks and look into her eyes. I didn't want to. She spanked me with the hairbrush she had brought with her. In the photograph I am standing with my hands on her face, looking at her as I was told to do. I remember hating her. She used to spank me a lot with her hairbrush and I realized, after I was grown up, that she probably derived a sexual pleasure from it. I remember her flushed face, quickened breathing, sparkling eyes. Afterward, Ma would take me into her own bedroom, pat Vaseline on my little red bottom, hold me in her arms and comfort me, trying to quiet my sobbing. I used to imagine that I had my mother tied naked on a bed, spread-eagled, and that I would horsewhip her while she screamed. She had never been spanked or slapped, herself, when a child, just as my grandmother never punished me in any way or said a stern word to me. The worst she ever said to me was if I forgot to close the screen door and she would ask tartly, "Where were you brought up—in a sawmill?" Or, again, if I slurred the word "for," she would say teasingly, "What fur? Cat's fur to make kittens' breeches out of?" Indeed, there was little reason for anyone to punish me. I was an unnaturally good child. I never talked back, never disobeyed, never broke anything, did my lessons, always got A-plus and 100 in my school reports, did whatever housework I was told to do, ran errands, was a real Little Goody Twoshoes.

Excerpt from my diary when I was eight: "My Mama and my Daddy left for Europe again. Europe is so far away. You've nearly always been away from me, Mama." Excerpt when I was eleven: "Mama and Daddy were in Florida again for Christmas. Before they left, Mama told me that I was a forceps baby. That means the doctor used a thing like a big sugar tongs to grab my head and pull me out when I was born. He gave Mama chloroform and Mama says it's supposed to make the child feeble-minded so they don't use it any more. I don't think it made me feeble-minded or I couldn't get such good marks in school. Could I?"

I think I was being sentimental and self-pitying because I felt children were supposed to love their mothers and vice versa. I was really happy with my grandmother. We not only loved each other; we were friends and companions. When I was eight she put me in a private school in Syracuse and took an apartment there for us. She helped me with my homework, hired a French tutor for me, a Madame Fougeray with chalk-white false teeth, took me to swimming classes at the YWCA and to dancing classes. She taught me to "speak pieces" and wept with happy pride when I won the Poetry Banner for the Best Speaker at Commencement every year. Until I was eleven, she dressed me every morning. In the winter she would spit on my feet because I couldn't stand the dry feeling of my black cotton stockings, and she would wrap the long wool legs of my union suit carefully under my stockings so they wouldn't itch, attach the stocking tops to the garter pins on my under vest and button my high black shoes with a buttonhook. She was never impatient or bad-tempered. Occasionally, she displayed a streak of unexpectedly black humor, as when she recited to me a verse from her own childhood that went: "Little Willie in the best of sashes/Fell in the fire and burned to ashes./ Now, whenever the room gets chilly/We take a poker and stir up Willie." I fell about with laughter and she looked worried. "Heavens to Betsy!" she said. "What a thing for me to tell you. Promise me that you'll forget it this very minute." Of course I never did.

Occasionally, I went to visit my parents in Syracuse or New York and I couldn't wait to get back to Ma. I suspect they felt the same way. When I was seven I spent about six months with them in New York, where we lived in a hotel. Kitty Gordon, an actress famous for her beautiful back and shoulders, lived in the same hotel and sometimes we saw her in the elevator. Percy Hammond, a brilliant drama critic, wrote of her appearance in some play, "her icy arms, white as the cliffs of Dover and just as formidable." A few years later I saw her in a movie, possibly the only one she ever made. She played a World War I nurse. There was a terrifying scene where the German soldiers rushed into an Allied hospital and these horrible Huns tore the bandages off the wounded. Fortunately, it was a silent film and in black and white.

I was far more frightened when my parents took me to the Chamber of Horrors in the old Eden Musee (pronounced *mu-zee*). After more than sixty years I still remember one dreadful waxwork of an elephant lifting a foot up and down, squashing a Negro's head, and another one where a man was being tortured, his arms and legs pulled out of the sockets, complete with simulated gore. When we left, I was limp and could scarcely walk. My mother and father had to support me as we made our way to the trolley.

During that New York period I went to the Ethical Culture school, where we sat at small wooden desks with built-in inkwells. We wrote with pens with steel nibs that fitted into the wooden pen handles. I wrote my grandmother every day and still have one of these notes, written May 26, 1915. The scrawl says: "Dear Ma: It is a great honor to the child who gets 100 in arithmetic. I won it. Baby." I enclosed my arithmetic paper.

My father took me to and from school. We rode in streetcars open on both sides, with rows of benches that stretched crosswise. You just hopped on wherever you saw a vacant place on a bench. I was the only Gentile child in my class but I didn't realize it because I didn't know the difference. There was an older girl named Leona who befriended me. One day after school she was walking with me and my father. Suddenly she asked me, "What is your religion?" "Episcopalian, of course," I answered. A few steps farther, it struck me as an odd question. "What religion are you?" I asked. She smiled. "Jewish, of course," she said.

When I was eleven I spent a week of my Christmas vacation in New York. My parents took me to the Hippodrome, where Charles Dillingham was presenting *Cheer Up*, a historical pageant from Columbus to Admiral Dewey, via Pocahontas, Barbara Fritchie and Teddy Roosevelt, with "300 chorus girls and music by John Philip Sousa," as the program said. This was in December 1911. The Hippodrome boasted of 5,697 seats, of which the highest priced were two dollars. We sat down front in the first row. All I can remember of the show were several elephants—in connection with what I have no idea—and an act called "The Submarine Belles. The Disappearing Divers—Where Do They Go?" These were girls dressed in black Annette Kellerman swim suits, like leotards, covering feet and legs as well as torsos. They dove into a large tank of water on the stage and never came up.

When I was twelve, I spent part of my Easter vacation with my mother at the Marlborough-Blenheim Hotel in Atlantic City— where we rode horseback and went to a Fun Palace, at which she made me get in a large bowl that spun round and round, faster and faster, as I got sicker and sicker. They didn't stop the machine until I threw up. I've always hated fun parks ever since. However, I apparently enjoyed the rest of the holiday in New York. One entry in my diary reads: "We had lunch at the Ritz-Carlton Hotel. This evening we went to see Raymond Hitchcock in *Hitchy Koo*. It was wonderful. The costumes were gorgeous! They must have cost a lot. Ermine coats, glittering metallic dresses, peacock feathers. All sumptuous. I sat right next to the runway. Words cannot express it. Florence O'Denishawn danced superbly. Hitchy came down in the audience. He shook hands with Daddy and Mama. He was giving away dolls and he asked me if I wanted one. I said, 'No.' He said, 'Oh, excuse me! *Faux pas*. An automobile for *her!*' I shall never forget it as long as I live. Mama wore her white satin dress with silver stockings and silver shoes. I wore my best party dress, white taffeta with pink roses and panels of pink tulle ruffles, white silk stockings and black Mary Janes. We dress for dinner every night."

In Syracuse my grandmother took me to the theater once a week and at least once a week to the movies. Many of the silent-screen stars had names like Louise Lovely, Grace Darling, Blanche Sweet, Arline Pretty, Bessie Love, Elinor Fair, Leatrice Joy. My favorite was Marguerite Clark, whom I liked better than Mary Pickford. I also admired the stately and ladylike Elsie Ferguson, the two Gish sisters, the three Talmadge sisters and Pauline Frederick, whom Ma and I saw in that perennial weepie *Madame X*, later remade by Ruth Chatterton and eventually by Lana Turner. I saw Elmo Lincoln in the first Tarzan film. I loved all the Tarzan books, although after I was grown up and began to read them to my small son, I was indeed surprised to find that in the original book Tarzan, visiting England and France after he learned he was Lord Greystoke, smoked cigarettes, drank absinthe and had an affair with a married woman in Paris. This was not the pure and noble Tarzan of later comic books.

My grandmother was as great a movie fan as I was. She bought me movie magazines and gave me money to send away for photographs of our favorites. I was crazy about Mabel Normand, a hoydenish, fun-loving girl who took dope and died of it. Hollywood was full of scandals in silent-film days, of which Ma and I were unaware for the most part. Dope, wild love affairs, rapes, suicides and several officially unsolved murders, although it was known who committed them. Yet all the participants maintained a public image of clean-cut boyishness in the men and wide-eyed, curl-tossing ingenue purity in the girls, even if some of them had the same uncomfortably innocent look as kittens dressed in overalls and photographed for the Sunday paper brown rotogravure sections. In retrospect, their vices seem more beguilingly ingenuous than the neuroticism of today, but that may be the gloss of memory. They had kinetic, extravagant personalities, and they came to fame and riches the hard way. Many of them started work at the age of four or five. Bebe Daniels at four was touring the country as the Duke of York in *Richard III* and made her movie debut at five in *The Squaw Man*. At thirteen she starred opposite Harold Lloyd as his leading lady in the Lonesome Luke two-reel comedies. . . . Mary Pickford, "America's Sweetheart," born Gladys Smith, whose grandparents emigrated to Canada from County Kerry in Ireland, was playing two parts in the stage play *The Sil-*

ver King, when she was five. Her only schooling was one winter when she was six. When she was eight, she toured in a play with her mother, her sister Lottie, then seven, and her brother Jack, five. They were paid twenty dollars a week for all four of them, playing one-night stands throughout Canada. By the time she was thirteen, she was alone in New York, looking for work. When she was fifteen she was starring at the old Biograph studios, making one picture a day. They were one-reelers, and she herself wrote many of the scripts.

They were not the overnight successes to which we are accustomed today. They were tough and gutsy people who worked hard and played hard. Their films may look ridiculous now but no more so, I think, than many of the Thirties pictures so canonized by modern movie buffs. The so-called Hollywood "greats" of the Thirties were personalities but not actors. Serious critics didn't consider them great even in their heyday. I know. I was there. With a few honorable exceptions, most of the films they made had silly dialogue and awful acting. I deplore the tendency to imitate them. Even as a child I never thought a custard pie thrown in a face was funny. I thought it was revolting and I still do. Nor did I enjoy the automobile chases which I find just as boring today as I did then.

After I went away to boarding school at Bradford, near Boston, my close companionship with my grandmother broke up, although she was still the person who loved me most and in whose eyes I was always Right and Beautiful and Smart. I wrote her several times a week and spent my Christmas holiday with her in LaFargeville and my summer vacation with her on the St. Lawrence. She was the force that shaped me, and whatever I was, up to that date, she had influenced and sponsored. She was always my unfailing refuge. Anything I asked of her she gave me with joy in the giving, asking no thanks, no return. Until her final illness she was never sick. As long as I said my prayers I bargained for her immortality. Please, God, never let Ma die, and I'll do thus and so. Because I would never let myself think of the possibility of her death, I grew to think that she would live on and on. She herself expected to live to be one hundred. At the end, her fight for life was heroic, and she just missed winning.

Shortly after our marriage in 1931, my first husband, Heinz, and

I were staying with Ma at the summer place, when she suddenly became ill with what turned out to be pneumonia. We couldn't get a doctor on the island, and I rowed across the river at midnight to locate one. We took care of her for two days before we could get a nurse. The doctor said she hadn't a chance. My mother came up from New York and into the house like a volcano: supervising orgies of house cleaning, taking charge, ordering everyone around, with Ma stretched out helpless on the bed, gaunt and unsightly and game as hell. "Rats! There's nothing wrong with me. I'm just lazy," she said, but she was too weak to move. The day before she became sick she had spaded her rose garden, helped with the ironing and baked a great apple pie. She was nearly eighty-five and apparently in perfect health.

On the doctor's advice and my mother's insistence, we moved her by ambulance to LaFargeville. She put up a fight against this, declaring she wasn't dead yet. Or, rather, what she was said was, "I haven't kicked the bucket yet and I won't ride in an ambulance." She managed to get to her feet and then crumpled on the floor and had to be carried downstairs on a stretcher, tears rolling down her cheeks, muttering "Old fool!" to herself. She knew she would never come back. She had lived her life for other people: for her husband, who had huge walrus mustaches and drank from mustache cups on which Ma painted roses and violets; for my mother; and the last twenty-four years for me. Now she was stricken down, unable even to feed herself, waiting to die, perfectly conscious of what was happening. I sat by her side as much as I could, and her orange cat, Billy, slept on her bed, curled up by her neck, only taking time off to go out and catch chipmunks which he proudly brought to show her and for her to tell him what a smart boy he was. (Summers at the River, he often brought her live snakes which she had to kill with broom or spade.)

Although we had two nurses in LaFargeville, they didn't do any housework, nor did my mother. Heinz and I got the meals, did the dishes for the seven of us, did all the laundry, with from eighteen to twenty sheets in each wash, as poor Ma didn't always calculate correctly on the bedpan, and ran errands at everyone's beck and call. I was with Ma when she finally died, after hanging on for three gallant months. It was the first death I ever witnessed. The electric water pump broke down and I had to carry water from the hand pump to the undertaker, who was laying her out. Death does ghastly things to a face within a few hours and whereas with someone else I might have had a clinical interest, because it was Ma my reaction was one of great inner hysteria and panic, more pronounced because I had to be outwardly calm and efficient and sane. My mother took to her bed and had to be given sleeping powders, while Al, my stepfather, wasn't in much better shape. One of the nurses also broke down. She was a local woman who was fond of Ma and during Ma's last days would play hymns on our rosewood spinet, which Ma countered by trying to sing something that went "And the ladies in the vaudeville ride velocipedes in the vestibule. . . ." The big mahogany grandfather's clock also stopped, for the first time in my memory.

To me fell the task of helping the undertaker, notifying the relatives, making arrangements with the minister and the gravedigger, choosing the casket and the bearers and, not least, sitting up from two to five one morning with the corpse and a nurse during a thunderstorm, when the lights all went out and we sat there in Ma's bedroom with one candle burning. The nurse, a good Catholic, insisted on sitting up with the body both nights before the funeral, but she was afraid of thunderstorms and so was my mother, so the night of the storm I had to keep the nurse company in the eerie room. Heinz had gone back to New York and so had my stepfather. Callers to the house were scarcely given a chance to pay their respects to the body, because my mother overwhelmed them with voluble, nonstop accounts of how much *she* was suffering. After the funeral held in the living room, and the burial in the LaFargeville cemetery, my mother had to be waited on hand and foot. I stole away for an hour and went down in the cellar, where I sat by myself, weeping for the first time since it all began. I never wanted to go back to that house again.

* * *

It was a winter evening in Syracuse in November 1930. I had been walking fast and was tired. Breathless, I leaned against a fence and looked around me. There was a dark mist everywhere, as if a can of ashes had been sifted through the air and only their dull gray smoke remained. Perhaps it was the sharp whiteness of the snow that made the air and sky look soiled in comparison. The one tinge of color was a group of pale amethyst shadows huddled together in the western corner of the sky. A tall, thin, black street lamp cast its star glow on the straight, parallel lines of the trolley tracks which reached out over the snow. Behind me I could hear the grumbling of an approaching car, disturbing the silence. The air smelled cold and damp. The hard points of the fence began to hurt my back and I was shivering. As I moved on, I could feel the snow squash under my feet like wet meal, and my breath steamed out to mingle with the dingy air.

"I have been here long enough," I thought. Four years on Syracuse newspapers. It was time to move on. The next day I quit my job and headed for New York, leaving behind the lovers and the laughter, deliberately shutting out the memories. I never returned, except once, for my father's funeral in the Fifties. It has only been in the past few years, throwing away old diaries, letters and scrapbooks packed in trunks kept in storage, that I have mentally revisited the past, neither with nostalgia nor regret. Some of it I have written about in this book and in a previous one. A few critics have been shocked, which surprises me. I am not a salacious writer. I am truthful and outspoken, but not lascivious. I have been amazed by reviewers who have portrayed me as a onetime giddy, sex-mad ornament of café society in the Thirties. One woman writer patronizingly described me as a "madcap." I laughed out loud when I read that. I have supported myself since I was nineteen and have also supported various members of my family. I have been housewife and mother as well as breadwinner. Some madcap!

It is possible that part of the disapproval stems from my reputation as a lady tosspot. In my younger days I used to be a formidable drinker, perhaps due to the childhood inoculation with cherry bounce. I was a hard drinker but strictly a sociable one. I have never sought it as an anodyne. Some of my friends have been alcoholics but I was never one and never could be one. I have never gone in a bar or pub alone, except to keep an appointment, and the only times in my life I have ever had a drink by myself have been a drink before or after dinner on a ship, in a restaurant, or at a sidewalk café, usually while traveling on magazine assignments.

As I have written before, I was a Prohibition drinker. We drank hootch, bathtub gin (made of medicinal alcohol mixed with juniper berries) served with orange juice and called Orange Blossoms, and needled beer. I must have had a cast-iron stomach. I discovered tequila in Havana in 1932 and it is still my favorite drink, although I don't suppose I touch it more than a few times a year, and then usually to bolster my courage when I have to do an interview or give one myself or appear on radio or television. I am not an entertainer and I suffer from stage fright. I sympathize with Andy Warhol, who told me that when he is interviewed on television and the moment comes when they begin the countdown, he thinks, "Is this where I faint?" The first time I was ever interviewed was on radio in 1946. It was a New York talk show conducted by Shirley Wolfe, called "Celebrity at Midnight." It was live and it did take place at midnight. The celebrity that particular night was scheduled to be Joe Louis, but he was held up in Chicago and couldn't make it. I was picked as a last-minute substitute. (When I told my husband this, he said, "Well of course the first person anyone would think of to substitute for Joe Louis would be you!") The only guests in the studio were two FBI men from the Picatinny Arsenal in New Jersey who had come in the hope of meeting the heavyweight champion. I imagine they were pretty disappointed when Miss Wolfe opened the program by saying, "Unfortunately, Joe Louis is not able to be you with tonight. However, we have a delightful surprise for you. . . ." My mouth was dry, my hands sweaty, and I was sure I was going to faint and she would say, "Due to circumstances beyond our control you will now hear a Strauss waltz." Somehow, I managed to get through it. The FBI men gallantly invited me to go for a drink with them afterward, but I was a nursing mother at the time and had to rush home to my infant son. I wouldn't have gone with them anyway.

The most unusual drinking experience I've ever had, and one I am positive I will never repeat, was seven or eight years ago in Paris when an Icelandic painter, a friend of my daughter, took me to dinner. I innocently thought it was kind of him to show this courtesy to the elderly mother of one of his friends. We had some wine with dinner and when the coffee came I suggested cognac.

He said he had a surprise for me. He signaled the waiter, who brought a bottle wrapped in a napkin. From it he poured two drinks. I didn't particularly like the taste, which was very strong, but I drank it politely. Then the sculptor removed the napkin from the bottle. Coiled inside was a dead snake, its head reaching the neck of the tall bottle. I guess I was expected to scream and I certainly felt like it, but I didn't. The sculptor explained that small young vipers are put alive in bottles and fed sugar, with brandy gradually added. As the snakes grow, a tree branch is put in the bottle. The viper climbs the branch but can't get out of the bottle. He added the nauseating details that the vipers vomit and excrete into the brandy, and eventually, when the bottle is full, they die. The drink originated in Korea, where it is apparently popular, he said. He was watching me closely to see my reaction. I was determined not to give him any satisfaction. "All right. Let's have another one," I said. "But keep the napkin around the bottle."

I took a deep breath and downed the second drink. "Here I am," I thought, "an old lady in my sixties, drinking viper brandy with an Icelandic painter on the Left Bank of Paris." And, suddenly, I remembered my grandmother's cherry bounce. It had been a long trail from LaFargeville, a life of contrasts, something like a patchwork quilt, or crazy quilt, as my grandmother called them. She made me a beautiful one of varicolored silks and velvets from old family clothes, including her own plum-colored brocade wedding dress from June 1867. I wouldn't have wanted it all the same color or pattern, any more than I would have wanted my life to be that way. It hasn't been.

T